EXCEPT

LEADERSHI

16 Critical Competencies

for Healthcare Executives

EXCEPTIONAL LEADERSHIP

16 Critical Competencies

for Healthcare Executives

Carson F. Dye and Andrew N. Garman

Health Administration Press
Chicago, IL

Your board, staff, or clients may also benefit from this book's insight. For more information on quantity discounts, contact the Health Administration Press Marketing Manager at (312) 424-9470.

10   09   08   07   06   5   4   3   2   1

Library of Congress Cataloging-in-Publication Data
Dye, Carson F.
   Exceptional leadership: 16 critical competencies for health executives/Carson F. Dye and Andrew N. Garman.
   p. cm.
   Includes bibliographical references.
   ISBN-10: 1-56793-252-5
   ISBN-13: 978-1-56793-252-2

   1. Health services administration. 2. Leadership. 3. Medical care—Quality control. I. Garman, Andrew N. II. Title.

RA971.D94 2006
362.1068—dc22

                                                         2005055058

The paper used in this publication meets the minimum requirements of American National Standard for Information Sciences—Permanence of Paper for Printed Library Materials, ANSI Z39.48-1984. ∞ ™

Acquisitions manager: Audrey Kaufman; Project manager: Jane Calayag; Cover design: Robert Rush

Health Administration Press
A division of the Foundation of the
   American College of Healthcare Executives
1 North Franklin Street, Suite 1700
Chicago, IL 60606-3424
(312) 424-2800

Contents

CORNERSTONE 4: MASTERFUL EXECUTION

Acknowledgments

CARSON DYE'S ACKNOWLEDGMENTS

I OPEN WITH an acknowledgment of and praise for Andy Garman. Our mutual, keen interest in leadership led to our decision to work on a book together. While I felt I did not have the time to write another book, Andy's prodding and willingness to carry much of the load led us to this stage. Andy, thanks—I respect you.

I also note specific contributions from several colleagues who helped us identify the leadership competencies that appear in the book. I am indebted to them for their valuable insight and time; despite their busy schedules, they responded to my weekend e-mails. These individuals are Jim Gauss, Mike Doody, Christine Mackey Ross, Susan Nalepa, Karen Otto, Martha Hauser, and Jared Lock.

My work in executive search allows me to observe and assess leadership competencies almost every day. I have worked with many stellar leaders over the years who have modeled extraordinary leadership. They model the competencies presented in the book, and their organizations have reaped the positive outcomes. These exceptional leaders are Steve Mickus, Ed Curtis, Mike Covert, Gene Miyamoto,

Richard Parks, Tom Beeman, Scott Malaney, Rick Palagi, Chip Hubbs, Ken Bryan, and Bill Linesch.

A special acknowledgment is in order for healthcare leaders in the military. Although we see them at ACHE's annual Congress and at various seminars, we do not always realize what their work entails. I am greatly indebted to the many medical service corps leaders I have worked with over the years. Leading discussions with these wonderful men and women in uniform has been a true blessing. While there are far too many military healthcare leaders to list, I do want to especially acknowledge David Rubenstein, Paul Williamson, Mark Wilhite, Steve Eldridge, and Bill Head.

Through my career I have also been blessed with many individuals who helped me grow as a leader. They include Walter McLarty, Paul Palmisano, Randy Schimmoeller, Carol Cogossi, Gretchen Patton, Dr. Greg Taylor, and Dr. Ed Pike.

I am also deeply appreciative of my friends at Health Administration Press, especially Audrey Kaufman and Jane Calayag. We are very fortunate in our industry to have such a dedicated group who provides us with wonderful learning through their book offerings.

A final acknowledgment, and the most important, goes out to my family. My wife, Joaquina, is always supportive and is simply always there. She is solid and very loving, and I appreciate that so much. My daughters—Carly, Emily, Liesl, and Blakely—and my son-in-law, Jeremy, have been quite kind as well. The girls have endured many absences as I traveled and wrote. I acknowledge and recognize them. And a special thanks to Liesl for managing the models in the book.

ANDY GARMAN'S ACKNOWLEDGMENTS

I'D LIKE TO thank my wife, Deborah, and our children, Emily and Tyler, for their support, endurance, and tolerance while I pursued this obsession. Thanks also to my parents and grandparents for instilling a strong familial culture of rigorous critical thought and a respect for scientific inquiry. A special thanks to the role-model leaders who have contributed to the governance and leadership courses at Rush University's Health Systems Management Program: Jackie Bishop, Mike Doody, Rupert Evans, Larry Goodman, Diane Howard, Mary Katherine Krause, David Leach, Wayne Lerner, John Lloyd, Christine Malcolm, Diane McKeever, Dennis Millirons, Marie Sinioris, Nancy Spector, Jeremy Strong, and Jack Trufant.

Thanks also to the following people who strongly influenced my thinking on leadership as a developing scholar: Roya Ayman, Bart Craig, Bruce Fisher, Arthur Freedman, and Dick Kilburg. Thanks to my past and present colleagues in healthcare leadership research: Pat Corrigan, Lakeisha Daniel, Jodi Darnall, Deb Davis-Lenane, Matt Johnson, and Larry Tyler; I thank Denise Oleske, for tolerating my eminently non-NIH-fundable research interests for so many years, and Peter Butler, for reenergizing Rush's interest in leadership development. Thanks to ACHE for championing health administration as a profession. Another special thanks to the many leaders who have willingly contributed their time and expertise to the leadership research projects I have been involved with over the years.

This book also benefited tremendously from the editorial guidance of Audrey Kaufman, Jane Calayag, and their colleagues at Health Administration Press. Thank you so much for all your help and support.

Thanks, finally, to Carson Dye for building another bridge between practice and academia by agreeing to take this project on in the first place. Our opportunities to dialog, disagree, and find common ground are to me the greatest reward of our collaborative writing.

For my family—Joaquina, Carly, Emily, Liesl, Blakely, and Jeremy—always supportive during my absences and always my treasure.

For the many healthcare leaders in the field, often unsung but often demonstrative of these great leadership competencies.

Carson F. Dye

To the practitioner faculty of Health Systems Management at Rush University, who are leading by example for the next generation of healthcare executives. Some of the finest teachers and mentors in the world walk quietly among their ranks.

Andrew N. Garman

Foreword

IT HAS BEEN said that leadership is the art of taking risk; management is the science of mitigating it. In this superb book, *Exceptional Leadership: 16 Critical Competencies for Healthcare Executives*, authors Carson Dye and Andy Garman outline the areas that leaders need to improve on if they aspire to be extraordinary leaders. Truly the art of leadership, like any art, requires the discipline of practice and commitment to continued personal growth. As must a pianist play scales endlessly so that Mozart's music could someday flow from her fingertips, so must a leader follow principles of great stewardship everyday to make her leadership seem effortless.

As Dye and Garman point out through their insightful review of core competencies, it is through the prism of qualities such as living by personal conviction, communicating vision, mentoring others, and stimulating creativity that the true nature and character of a leader can evolve. The important word here is evolve. Although one may possess the innate talents required for visionary leadership, one has to hammer out such talents on the anvil of experience; otherwise these talents are useless, uninspiring, and inert. A leader becomes a leader when people are willing to follow. It is here in this mutuality that leaders find their dignity. Hebrew scripture says, "Without a vision the people perish," and without people to show the way, leadership is empty. A person's desire to lead without the willingness to work hard only results in meaningless leadership and disillusioned followers.

Dye and Garman have tailored their book to those who recognize that leadership is a talent to be cultivated and that to be a great leader one must sit at the feet of even greater ones to learn. Leadership is not an end point but a process of becoming that is worth working for, no matter how difficult. Especially useful in Dye and Garman's book are the interesting vignettes that set up the context for the ensuing discussion in the chapters. By demonstrating the utility and significance of say, emotional intelligence, the authors engage the readers more meaningfully in the discussion of the concepts. This engagement can lead the reader to enter into self-assessment, making this book not only an enjoyable read but also an immensely satisfying guide to successful leadership development.

Why leadership development, and why a healthcare leadership book? One has only to look around to see the ethical vacuum that has been created by lack of organizational leadership in American businesses. Combine that with a dearth in personal values and accountability, and you will find that America is in crisis. In healthcare, which is ever more a public trust, the need for transformational and ethical leaders is a paramount concern. Much of our healthcare crises have been caused by a focus on the economics and commoditization of healthcare rather than on the ethics and rights of healthcare.

Given this environment, Dye and Garman's work is timely. At a time when leadership is often mistaken for power (which subtly corrupts character), it is great to have a book that focuses on developing character, which is and must be the fundamental element of leadership.

—Thomas E. Beeman, CHE,
president and chief executive officer, Lancaster General,
Lancaster, Pennsylvania

Preface

THERE ARE GOOD leaders, then there are *exceptional leaders*. You are aware of this, although you may not be able to articulate how one is different from the other. You understand, however, that exceptional leaders are generally more successful, their message and performance have more impact, their plans better developed and implemented, and their legacy longer lasting. Furthermore, these leaders achieve more effective results, which helps perpetuate their extraordinary work and qualities.

The answer to, "What makes a leader exceptional?" is simple: competencies. Because the term "competencies" is explored in the Introduction, we present a simplified definition here. *Competencies* are a set of professional and personal skills, knowledge, values, and traits that guide a leader's performance, behavior, interaction, and decisions. Because leadership is a complex undertaking, it requires many competencies. "Many" is the operative word here, as various organizations have developed their own competency models and many leadership books discuss this concept.

"Many," however, does not sit well with extremely busy healthcare leaders. "Few but effective" do, as the list of 16 competencies in this book intends to prove. These competencies, a byproduct of our close work and association with healthcare leaders and search consultants, were selected because we have observed them to be factors that distinguish good leaders from exceptional leaders. In addition, each competency also appears in the competency models and on lists developed by healthcare organizations and consultants, including the Healthcare Leadership Alliance (2005) Competency Directory that was recently created by six major healthcare associations.

Any leadership book will tell you *how* to make a leader exceptional. This book offers that and an added advantage: it tells you *what* makes a leader exceptional. We define these competencies and fully discuss what they entail.

We assembled the competency list for three reasons:

1. Many good leaders in healthcare truly want to be great leaders, and they want it for the right reason—to make a genuine difference to the patients and communities they serve.
2. Most healthcare leaders do not have a wealth of mentors, do not continually attend many leadership programs, or are not presented with skill-development opportunities on a proverbial silver platter.
3. In this period often marked by the "war for talent," leaders need to be better equipped to assess the skills and competencies of other leaders, especially those they are hiring.

If you want to learn the distinguishing marks of more effective leadership, this book was written for you. Your knowledge will allow you to develop yourself and other leaders and make better hiring decisions for your organization.

WHY ANOTHER BOOK ON LEADERSHIP?

Healthcare Leadership Is Different

Many leadership issues are the same regardless of industry, but healthcare presents many unique challenges. The relationships, life-

and-death nature of the work, emotional demands, and financial challenges in this industry are very different from those in other fields. Because of these unique qualities, the healthcare field requires its leaders to have a distinctive approach as well, so the competencies in this book give leaders this edge.

Healthcare Is in Desperate Need of Great Leaders

The greatest challenge of the next decade in healthcare could very well be the development of leaders equipped to deal with the healthcare field, which is facing declining reimbursement, a complex tapestry of professional labor shortages, and the increasing sophistication and costs of medical technology. All of these challenges will continue in this high-stakes environment, where consumerism, malpractice, public reporting, or patient safety and quality concerns can change the course of a hospital's future in a heartbeat.

The Science of Leadership Is Evolving

Although great strides have been made in the past decade in the science of leadership assessment and development, extracting solid information from the leadership rhetoric remains very difficult. Bookstores are filled with books on leadership, but most of these books reflect the perspective of a single successful leader or author.

In this book, we marry the areas of leadership performance that need critical attention with the most current research in these areas. In this way, we provide the most advanced thinking on how to develop in these competencies.

Not All Leadership Competencies Are Equally Important

Leadership competency models are proliferating in health administration. Multiple consulting firms, healthcare organizations, and professional associations all have created their leadership competency lists. If every competency in every one of these models were added, they would quickly add up into the hundreds.

In our experience, long lists of competencies are fine for a job analysis but not at all helpful in planning for development. They are even less helpful when used as a way to discern the differences among candidates for leadership positions.

This is why we focus on just the 16 competencies that, in our and our colleagues' collective experience, seem to make the biggest difference between good leadership and great leadership. If your goal is to be an exceptional leader, these are the competencies you need to master. If you need help in developing better selection criteria when hiring, these competencies are the primary ones to use in assessment.

Leadership Development Is *Your* Responsibility

Exceptional leaders take responsibility for their own development. They do not wait for their superiors to guide them or for their organizations to sponsor events. If you want to be an exceptionally effective leader, it is up to you to learn your development needs and to find your own ways to improve.

WHAT CAN BE GAINED FROM READING THIS BOOK?

Our goal is to present the competencies that mark an exceptional leader. Throughout the book we offer tools to help good leaders develop their own capacity, that of their direct reports, and even that of their organization.

A Deeper Understanding of Leadership

By reading and reflecting on each of the 16 competencies, you will derive additional insight into leadership and a better understanding of the key qualities that drive highly effective leadership.

Guidance in Coaching and Developing Skills

This book provides practical suggestions for developing leadership skills that can immediately be implemented. You can use this book to plan your own development or to help others in planning their development. Executive coaches may use the material to help guide and shape the behavior of those they are coaching. Executives may find the discussion helpful in counseling and advising direct reports about their leadership behavior.

Guidelines in Assessing Executive Candidates

This book serves as an excellent guide in assessing candidates for executive leadership positions. The 16 competencies can be used as a benchmark to develop interview questions and to evaluate leadership capability.

Counsel on Avoiding Derailment

No one sets out to purposely derail his career. Still, career derailments often happen. Skill deficits in any of these areas can stall or even disrupt a leadership career. Understanding your own development needs can help you prevent derailing your own career.

A Foundation for Broader Leadership Competency Models

Because the competencies in this book focus on exceptional leadership, you may find them to be a useful springboard to develop competency models of your own.

A Practical Foundation for Teaching Leadership

The material in this book lends itself to use in academic instruction. For example, one use may be as a complement to theory-based texts. Competencies can be used as stand-alone topics, and the vignettes at the beginning of each chapter can serve as discussion starters. The self-assessment and development suggestions also lend themselves well to career-development planning assignments. Additionally, this book can serve as the foundation for peer-led leadership-development meetings in practice settings.

REFERENCE

Healthcare Leadership Alliance. 2005. Competency Directory. [Online information; retrieved 11/1/05.] www.healthcareleadership.alliance.org/directory.cfm.

Introduction

WE CAN ALL think of those who seem to have been born to lead. There are almost always at least a couple of such leaders in every hospital. They stand out because they give the impression that they can make things happen and that they are going to succeed at anything. We often determine the success of these leaders long before their performance results come in.

This kind of leadership can be learned by those who are not natural-born leaders. The road to becoming such a leader takes discipline, and it is much harder for some than for others. We firmly believe, however, that the practices, also known as *competencies* (see Exhibit 1), of exceptional leaders can be picked up by anyone.

Those in the position of selecting leaders can also benefit from learning about competencies. It will help them in their assessments of candidates and in their hiring decisions. A hiring mistake at the senior level is disastrous for any organization, and a better understanding of exactly what comprises highly effective leadership will minimize this risk.

Exhibit 1

What is a competency?

Many definitions of competencies exist, but the late David McClelland (1973) is widely regarded as providing the original and most authoritative definition. At the time of his writing, intelligence and skills tests were the main tools used to make selection decisions. McClelland's work was an attempt to move beyond a narrow, skills-focused definition of success to examine broader, underlying characteristics of individuals that could be used to predict success.

In brief, competencies include a broad collection of knowledge, skills, abilities, and characteristics. They include values (such as ethics and integrity), cognitive skills (such as thinking and problem solving), interpersonal skills (such as communicating and listening), embracing diversity (such as tolerance and respect), and change management (such as strategic planning and risk taking).

As deeper-level constructs, competencies are not something learned from a day-long training workshop or a class. They are more accurately described as improving slowly over time as a result of mindful practice, feedback, and more practice.

LEADERSHIP COMPETENCY MODEL

We organized this book around 16 leadership competencies. These are the competencies most associated with exceptional leadership in healthcare. We arrived at this list through the following steps:

1. We examined the competency lists prepared by boards and executives for use in their executive searches.
2. We pared this list down to those competencies that reliably differentiated the highest-performing leaders—people who made the short lists and who usually got hired.
3. We surveyed eight seasoned search consultants (with more than 100 collective years of search experience) who work exclusively in healthcare. We asked each of them the following questions:
   - What are the most important competencies your clients request when looking for new executives?

- Consider the three best executives you have ever placed in your search careers. Exactly what leadership competencies did these leaders have that set them apart from the others?

We retained the competencies submitted by multiple search consultants.

4. We posed similar questions regarding leadership competencies to healthcare chief executive officers (CEOs) and executive coaches.

5. To refine our conceptualizations of these 16 competencies, we compared and contrasted them with reviews of the academic leadership literature and competency lists of well-known consulting firms.

Our end goal was to develop a competency model focused enough to help aspiring exceptional leaders zero-in on their greatest development opportunities and rich enough to be revisited many times in the years to come.

We have organized these competencies into four traits, which we call the cornerstones of exceptional leadership:

Cornerstone 1: Well-cultivated self-awareness
Cornerstone 2: Compelling vision
Cornerstone 3: Real way with people
Cornerstone 4: Masterful style of execution

These cornerstones anchor our leadership model on the foundation of having a healthy self-concept, which is discussed later in this introduction. Figure 1 illustrates this foundation model.

AN OVERVIEW OF THE FOUR CORNERSTONES

Cornerstone 1: Well-Cultivated Self-Awareness

Self-awareness means understanding yourself as a leader—in particular, your strengths, limitations, hot buttons, and blind spots.

Figure 1

Developing self-awareness requires leaders to intellectually and emotionally process on two levels. First, leaders must develop the ability to collect accurate, high-quality feedback from the work environment. Second, leaders must contemplate with an open mind what that feedback means to them and to their performance as a leader.

While these processes sound deceptively simple, in reality they are far from simple. We all receive some feedback from the environment, and we all accept it with some open mindedness. The magnitude of both this environment and our capacity for being open minded makes the difference between good leadership and exceptional leadership. Exceptional leaders make sure their environment is rich in feedback (see Appendix E for suggestions on how to develop a feedback-rich environment) and internalize the feedback they receive.

High performance in the area of self-awareness also involves mastery of two competencies: living by personal conviction and possessing emotional intelligence. You can think of personal conviction as the driving force that guides you in serving a larger purpose; emotional intelligence, in contrast, involves the management of that purpose in the relationships you forge.

Cornerstone 2: Compelling Vision

Of the four cornerstones, a compelling *vision* tends to be both the most visible and the most closely associated with senior leadership roles. At the senior level, if leaders hit their ceilings before reaching their career goals, it is usually because they have not mastered one or more of the competencies in this cornerstone.

There are three competencies comprising this cornerstone associated with exceptional leadership: being visionary, communicating vision, and earning loyalty and trust.

Being visionary is the heart of this cornerstone and begins this section of the book. Vision can be defined as the capacity to create effective plans for your organization's future, based on a clear understanding of trends, uncertainties, risks, and rewards. Defined in this way, we can separate creation of vision from the process of building awareness and understanding of the vision (i.e., communicating vision) as well as gaining support from the "unconverted" (i.e., earning loyalty and trust).

Cornerstone 3: Real Way with People

This cornerstone relates to implementation—making things happen through people and through process.

Interpersonal relations are a central part of the leader's role, and most leaders who have been around a while already have a reasonably well-developed set of interpersonal skills. At a minimum, most leaders recognize that you can catch more flies with honey than with vinegar, that people care about more than just their paycheck, and that interpersonal conflicts rarely go away on their own. That said, our experience leads us to conclude that (1) outstanding leaders typically have outstanding interpersonal skills, and (2) most leaders have at least some room for growth in the area of interpersonal relations.

The interpersonal domain can be meaningfully split into five competencies: listening like you mean it, giving feedback, mentoring others, developing champion teams, and energizing staff.

In each case, our focus is on how to refine an already strong skill set to the level of outstanding performance. We begin this section with a chapter on listening, which in many ways is the central unifying characteristic of this cornerstone. In describing what makes an executive effective, Peter Drucker (2004) identified eight practices and just one rule: "Listen first, speak last."

Cornerstone 4: Masterful Style of Execution

The final cornerstone turns to an examination of *execution*—where the rubber meets the road in getting activities assigned to strategies, decisions made, tasks accomplished, and agendas moved forward.

Leaders are ultimately judged in terms of what they get done. Regardless of the leadership competencies they exhibit, the true measure of their impact is the success they bring to their organizations.

Although success in execution is strongly affected by the quality of a leader's working relationships, it is also affected by the approaches the leader uses. The six competencies that most distinguish the highest performing leaders in this domain are generating informal power, building consensus, making decisions, driving results, stimulating creativity, and cultivating adaptability. We examine each of these in turn.

HOW IS THIS BOOK STRUCTURED?

Each of the 16 competencies is explored in its own stand-alone chapter. Each chapter is organized around the following sections:

- *Opening vignette.* This section provides an example of the type of situation in which leaders can shine if they demonstrate a mastery of the competency.
- *Definition of the competency.* This section explains what the competency is and why it is so important.
- *When highly effective leaders demonstrate the competency.* Here

we describe, in specific details, what extraordinary leadership looks like when the competency is mastered.

- *When the competency is not all it could be.* Here we describe the common skill deficits that prevent good leaders from being great leaders in this competency.
- *Misuse and overuse: how the competency can work against you.* Sometimes leaders get into trouble because they overdo it. Here we describe what problems can arise for overdoing or misusing a given competency.
- *Finding role models.* One of the very best ways to learn new skills is to find a master to help you. In this section, we tell you where you are most likely to find people who have mastered the competency.
- *Additional opportunities for personal development.* Not all leadership development is equally effective. Here we provide options for developing a competency area, focusing on what has been shown to work best and what our colleagues and clients tell us have been most helpful to them.

Appendixes

In the appendixes, we have assembled a wealth of additional tools to help you along the path of personal development, including the following:

- A self-assessment questionnaire and scoring guide for each of the competencies
- A sample self-development plan
- An action plan for developing a feedback-rich working environment
- An action plan for implementing a 360-degree feedback program

Appendix A provides a set of self-reflection questions, which can help you prioritize your development by assessing your strengths and development needs. Appendix B provides a framework for structuring, implementing, and monitoring your leadership self-development plan.

Throughout this book, we make the case for finding and using mentors in developing your skills. Appendix C provides specific guidance on how to best approach mentors for their help and, once they have agreed to work with you, how to gain the maximum benefit from their experience and skills. For those of you in a position to avail yourself of professional mentoring, Appendix D provides guidelines for identifying and screening executive coaches as well as ensuring you are in the best position to benefit from what they have to offer.

Because most leadership skill development comes through practice, we also repeatedly make the case for ensuring you receive the most useful feedback available in your environment. Appendix E details how to cultivate a feedback-rich organizational climate using a variety of techniques. Lastly, Appendix F provides a decision-making framework and reviews the 360-degree feedback process for developmental purposes.

SELF-CONCEPT: THE FOUNDATION

As do real cornerstones, the four cornerstones of exceptional leadership must rest on a firm foundation. In the case of leadership, this foundation is a healthy self-concept.

The Critical Importance of Self-Concept

To be an exceptional leader and to perform at a superior level, it is essential that you have a healthy *self-concept*. Having a healthy self-concept means you agree with each of the following:

- You are satisfied with your place in the world and feel that you have a purpose in life.
- You feel a sense of control over your life and destiny.
- You are confident in your ability to achieve what you set out to do.
- You have a positive self-image.
- You feel comfortable with how you relate to others.

More simply, self-concept is your own understanding of and comfort level about yourself. Some people may refer to self-concept as self-esteem, or self-confidence, or self-value. Regardless of the terminology, the message is the same: If you are content and happy with who you are and what you have accomplished, you are comfortable with others as well and are fully accepting of their achievements and contributions, regardless of whether those contributions may be deemed to be of higher value than yours.

We are disappointed in the lack of attention that this subject receives. Most leadership development courses and their content material focus principally on behaviors and competencies. The reality is that without a healthy self-concept, the other leadership competencies at best will feel unnatural and at worst will never be mastered.

In the words of one well-known CEO, "I can usually tell more about leaders and their potential through learning how they perceive themselves than in any other way." Leaders with a positive self-concept do not have to tear down others to bring themselves up. They rarely yell, scream, or curse, and they do not feel the need to play political games for their own gain. Their value systems engender a positive regard for others because they first have a high, but appropriate, regard for themselves.

We consider positive self-concept a prerequisite for exceptional leadership because it influences every aspect of a leader's effectiveness. Self-concept makes its most visible difference in the way leaders handle success and failure and work with others.

Successes and Failures

While highly effective leaders are driven to achieve, they are in control of that drive. They enjoy their accomplishments and take pride in them. Failures and setbacks may bother them but do not tear them apart.

Leaders with a poor self-concept view accomplishments as simple milestones—expected points of passage on the way to other landmarks. They rarely see the value of praise given to their organization or community. These leaders are often said to be out to prove something.

A similar phenomenon occurs with failures. Leaders with high self-regard view their failures in a balanced fashion—sure, there is pain in failing, but there is also the opportunity to learn from mistakes. Failures will not cause great leaders to retreat from daring decisions in the future; instead, they will continue to move boldly but do so in a better-informed manner. Leaders with low self-regard do not see failures in the same way. They blame failures on others and on bad luck, and they seldom learn from such mistakes.

Working with Others

The more accepting leaders are of themselves, the better they are at accepting others. A leader's capacity to accept others creates a climate of psychological safety in the workplace. A safe climate allows people to better receive and use constructive feedback because they will not be distracted by feelings of personal vulnerability. Conversely, if people feel that their job is at risk, they are far more likely to act defensively, with self-preservation as their primary goal and the good of the team or organization as a secondary consideration.

A healthy self-concept also lends itself to encouraging and embracing diversity in the workplace. We have found that those who have a solid self-concept are more tolerant and accepting of people who have different backgrounds and beliefs. One of the hallmarks of exceptional leadership is the willingness and ability to assemble teams made up of diverse individuals. These leaders know that there is a great advantage to having such a team. Today's great leaders must continually incorporate diversity initiatives into their strategies; a strong self-concept makes doing this much easier.

Make no mistake: leaders can go very far *without* a healthy self-concept. We have observed several leaders who possess a low sense of self-worth but still reach top positions in healthcare. They may even be successful throughout their entire careers. In fact, some are driven overachievers, and others are absolute perfectionists or are compulsively controlling. However, these leaders' achievements typically come at the expense of others. They use tactics such as fear, intimidation, and political manipulation that can tear at the fabric of an otherwise positive organizational culture. Their direct reports are unlikely to reach their full potential, and there are limits on how far people will follow these kinds of leaders.

We are clearly not alone in this perspective. A stream of research has been emerging that links self-regard to effectiveness. Several recent studies have found significant connections between self-concept (termed "core self-evaluations" in academia) and both job performance and job satisfaction (Judge and Bono 2000). Perhaps even more telling is that self-concept may also determine how much mentoring leaders receive during their career (Hezlett 2003), how effectively leaders can hear and use feedback on their performance (Bono and Colbert 2005), and how capable leaders are to recognize and pursue strategic opportunities on behalf of their organizations (Hiller and Hambrick 2005).

What to Do If Your Self-Concept Is Low

If you do not see this foundation in yourself, we recommend that you make building your self-concept a top priority. That may very well mean putting this book aside for a while or at least not beginning with these competencies as your primary focus. A positive self-concept is not something you can get from a book. However, we can suggest some useful first steps.

Consider How You Feel About Yourself

Are you satisfied with your life? Do you enjoy who you are, or do you have a nagging sense of regret? What about your career? Do you feel good about your achievements, or bad about the opportunities you may have missed out on? When you accomplish something, can you take pride in it, or do you view every achievement as nothing more than a means toward some greater end? When you fail at something, can you accept the lessons learned, or do you just curse yourself for trying in the first place? When someone else fails you, are you able to see their side, or do you find yourself quickly turning against them? If you were to learn that this day was your last, would you feel you had spent your life well?

The greater your personal discomfort with yourself, the more room you have to grow in the area of self-concept, and the more likely it is that this development should be your first priority.

Ask Those Closest to You for Their Candid Feedback
Consult a spouse, significant other, family member, or spiritual confidante to seek their opinion of your self-concept. Listen to them with an open mind, and try to take what they say at face value. Often, the people who know us well know us better than we know ourselves. Remember also that perceptions are often more important than reality.

Build on Your Positive Qualities
Build a focus on your positive physical, mental, and emotional qualities. What are you good at? What do you do well? What do you like about yourself? Use these positive concepts to counterbalance the aspects you feel less positive about. Enumerate your accomplishments. Celebrate achievements. Congratulate yourself on things you do well.

Seek to Understand Your "Dark" Side
Having a healthy self-concept does not mean that you have no sore spots or hot buttons. But it does mean that you know your vulnerabilities so that you can prevent them from undermining you. Understanding your "dark" side requires the discipline to face your vulnerabilities, to examine how they have interfered with your effectiveness in the past, and to learn how to spot the warning signals and what to do when you see them.

Enlist Some Help
Unlike the other competencies in this book, self-concept may *not* work as well as a self-development project. Professional assistance from a coach, spiritual counselor, therapist, or other professional with specialized training can make a big difference in the speed of your progress.

Exhibit 2

Is a competent leader an effective leader?

Not necessarily. Competence is most accurately described as the *capacity* to perform. To translate competency into *actual* performance requires both motivation and opportunity. Putting in the time and energy required for success requires motivation; we all face barriers to success, but exceptional leaders overcome these barriers more often. Opportunity relates to the environment in which leadership takes place; some environments are conducive to successful leadership, while others are not. We have seen exceptional leaders enter organizations and then leave because the environments were not set up to allow them to be successful.

That noted, our experience tells us you do get what you give. If you put the time and effort in, you can become a more successful leader. In the process, your ability to help others and your organization will expand along with your influence. In short, it is time well spent.

A FINAL WORD

With a mastery of these competencies, you will have the capacity to be an effective leader; however, you should expect the process to take considerable time and effort (see Exhibit 2). To master these leadership competencies, you will need to invest time to reflect on how you practice each competency. You may also need to develop and maintain reliable and accurate feedback mechanisms in your workplace. You will also need to master the ability to maintain your ground during times of substantial turbulence.

We wish you the best on your self-development and your career, and we hope you find this book to be a helpful guide along the way.

REFERENCES

Bono, J. E., and A. E. Colbert. 2005. "Understanding Responses to Multi-Source Feedback: The Role of Core Self-Evaluations." *Personnel Psychology* 58: 171–203.

Drucker, P. F. 2004. "What Makes an Effective Executive?" *Harvard Business Review* 82 (6): 58–63.

Hezlett, S. A. 2003. "Who Receives Mentoring? A Meta-Analysis of Employee Demographic, Career History, and Individual Differences Correlates." Unpublished doctoral dissertation, University of Minnesota, Minneapolis.

Hiller, N. J., and D. C. Hambrick. 2005. "Conceptualizing Executive Hubris: The Role of (Hyper-) Core Self-Evaluations in Strategic Decision-Making." *Strategic Management Journal* 26: 297–319.

Judge, T. A., and J. E. Bono. 2000. "Relationship of Core Self-Evaluation Traits—Self-Esteem, Generalized Self-Efficacy, Locus of Control, and Emotional Stability—With Job Satisfaction and Job Performance: A Meta-Analysis." *Journal of Applied Psychology* 86 (1): 80–92.

McClelland, D. C. 1973. "Testing for Competence Rather Than 'Intelligence'." *American Psychologist* 28 (1): 1–14.

CORNERSTONE 1

Well-Cultivated
Self-Awareness

CHAPTER ONE

Living by
Personal Conviction

Kevin awoke suddenly at 2:45 a.m., thinking again about the search for the hospital's new chief operating officer (COO). As president of a hospital that had grown too big for its management structure, Kevin was eager to bring someone on to take over many of the operating responsibilities so he could focus some much needed attention on community relations and fundraising. The hospital had been struggling to stay out of the red, and operations had been taking up far too much of Kevin's energies for several years.

The hospital was far along in the search process and had narrowed the field to two candidates: Tom and Lisa. Kevin had involved his executive team members in the interview process and wanted to allow them significant input. Kevin believed Tom was the right person for the job. Although he would be new to the COO role, he had experience as VP of operations in a comparably sized facility. A creative thinker, Tom displayed a clear sense of urgency and personal commitment to excellence, and he was able to drive very impressive results. Kevin knew Tom would do whatever was necessary to make the hospital run as efficiently as possible. This was evident in his accomplishments and was confirmed by his references.

The only problem? No one on Kevin's executive team favored Tom.

In Tom's interviews with the executives, he made it clear he saw his role in terms of hospital performance. While he intended to deal with people fairly, he was not afraid to let people go if he thought it would serve the needs of the hospital. The executives felt threatened by Tom.

When it became clear Kevin was favoring Tom, staff reacted by rallying around Lisa. Unlike Tom, Lisa already had the COO title on her résumé. She also had more years of work experience. During her onsite interview, she had done a far better job of establishing rapport with the team— everything from learning about their career goals to finding out about their history with the organization. She expressed accolades for the work the group had done and tremendous optimism in what could be accomplished in the future. But Lisa had her own limitations. She lacked Tom's sense of urgency, and her approaches tended to involve incremental changes rather than outside-the-box transformational ones. The level of results she achieved reflected this—acceptable but not particularly stellar. In short, while Lisa would probably do fine in the role, Tom would clearly do better.

Kevin's entire leadership team was against him on this one. A number of them had made veiled threats about leaving if Tom was hired. One had insinuated Kevin was being sexist in his decision. All were waiting for him to make an announcement that morning.

In this vignette, we find Kevin grappling with a tough decision involving, among other elements, competing values. The setting, a middle-of-the-night awakening, is one during which internal conflicts are often most apparent. The distractions and intrusions of the workday are there only as memories, which allows the real internal struggles to come forward.

WHAT IS LIVING BY PERSONAL CONVICTION, AND WHY IS IT IMPORTANT?

Living by personal conviction is the competency closest to the core of what a leader is. The highest-performing leaders we have encountered all share the following trait: They are strongly driven by their personal convictions. These convictions suggest to them how the world should be. They conceptualize their leadership role as moving them from their existing worlds to their ideal worlds. Personal conviction is closely linked to vision, another important leadership competency, which is discussed in Chapter 3.

> **Living by personal conviction** means you know and are in touch with your values and beliefs, are not afraid to take a lonely or unpopular stance if necessary, are comfortable in tough situations, can be relied on in tense circumstances, are clear about where you stand, and will face difficult challenges with poise and self-assurance.

For exceptional leaders, the source of strong personal conviction is derived from various sources, including religious beliefs, deeply held connections to community, and a very fundamental sense of morality—that is, what is right and wrong. All of these values are often, though not always, instilled at a very early age by very important caregivers. More than merely a compass, personal conviction provides leaders with the strength to carry on at times when they may feel they are the only person behind a cause or a goal. Perhaps most importantly, the strength of personal convictions helps highly effective leaders deal with setbacks and professional disappointments.

WHEN HIGHLY EFFECTIVE LEADERS LIVE BY PERSONAL CONVICTION

Everyone has some sense of personal conviction or some unifying set of principles by which they live. Decision making of any kind would not be possible in its absence—without a standard or metric by which to judge options, one option would never prevail over another one. Exceptional leaders, however, more consistently incorporate their personal conviction into their decisions. Several qualities of these leaders are outlined below.

Demonstrating Conviction

Highly effective leaders with strong personal conviction are people who demonstrate their moral and ethical principles through the work they do. They know their values and beliefs and are comfortable discussing them. Their peers and direct reports, if asked, would describe these leaders with phrases such as "highly principled," "standing for what they believe in," and "walking their talk."

Keeping Conviction in Check

While these highly effective leaders hold powerful convictions, they are also able to keep them appropriately in check. In addition, although they feel their convictions throughout their work, they are simultaneously able to recognize their convictions as personal and not universal. They are willing to blend the views and convictions of others into their decisions. They recognize their beliefs as "right for me" but not right in the absolute sense. While they may take delight in sharing their views, they are not overzealous missionaries out to convert their direct reports and peers. They view others' efforts to find their own individual larger purposes as virtuous in their own right, seeing this process as actually more important than the conclusions that are drawn.

Having Ethics

Highly effective leaders are usually well known for having high integrity and ethics. They understand there is an ethical dimension to most decisions, and they are not afraid to ensure ethical considerations are addressed before a decision is implemented.

WHEN LIVING BY PERSONAL CONVICTION IS NOT ALL IT COULD BE

Less effective leaders do not use their conviction to its fullest potential. As a source of guiding light, conviction may occasionally serve as a flashlight when a beacon is needed. It may affect thinking but fail to guide decision making. It may steer leaders in a virtuous direction at first but will ultimately lose out to outside pressures. Following are some common reasons that living by conviction falls short.

Having Internal Conflicts

While leadership roles inevitably involve compromise, leaders who lack strong personal conviction may find that the course their organization is following frequently shifts direction. They may agree to one direction in a physician meeting and then reverse the direction when under pressure from board members. Other times, they may sacrifice individual goals for the good of the team, and the team for the good of the organization. They may hold social goals at arm's length when there is a fiscal crisis in the hospital and the argument used is "no margin, no mission." The sheer pace of decisions and trade-offs in a leadership role can leave a leader little time for reflection and integration to the point where she begins to lose her sense of identity and becomes uncertain about her own beliefs.

Lacking Conviction

Some leaders cope with their personal compromises through avoidance. They tell themselves their ideals are not so important, or they avoid thinking about these ideals entirely. For others, the conviction may not have been strong to begin with. As they progress in their careers, these leaders do little to cultivate their beliefs, assuming "it [their life] is easier that way."

In well-run organizations, leaders can be focused on personal beliefs and still make substantial organizational contributions. Well-designed incentives and careful monitoring can keep personal beliefs well enough in line that organizational goals are not sacrificed. However, such leaders do not perform to their full potential. Their direct reports view their relationships as transactional and have little incentive to work past the point of expected accomplishment.

Having a Disconnect Between Conviction and Work

Other leaders have strong personal convictions but choose not to allow these convictions to be expressed in their work roles, or they fail to see the opportunities to support their convictions through their work. We have seen many such leaders—all talented individuals—halt themselves at mid-level roles, gradually diminishing their

When Living by Personal Conviction Is Not All It Could Be

The following are often the reasons that personal conviction is not as strong as it could be:

- Having internal conflicts
  - Leaders are uncertain about their own beliefs.
  - The organization's course frequently switches direction.
  - Individual goals are often sacrificed for the good of the team.

- Lacking conviction
  - Leaders either ignore or do not cultivate personal convictions.
  - Direct reports view their relationships with the leader as transactional.

- Having a disconnect between conviction and work
  - Leaders fail to see opportunities to support their personal convictions in their work.
  - There is too much focus on non-work outlets and too little focus on work.

- Overfocusing on personal goals
  - Staff lack a desire to help others.
  - Leaders view their position primarily as a vehicle for personal achievement.

focus on work while increasing their commitment to outside activities. They may champion great social causes, such as starting and running volunteer organizations, while at work they contribute at a reasonable but not superior pace.

Even more troubling are leaders who simply give up on thinking they can make a difference in their organizational roles. In this category, we find leaders who are experiencing executive burnout—those who may have had admirable but unrealistic ideas about what they could achieve in their senior roles but who find they are unable to recalibrate their expectations and fully engage in the considerable good they *can* accomplish. They have truly "retired on the job."

Overfocusing on Personal Goals

A final area where personal conviction can be detrimental involves allowing personal goals to become the be-all, end-all *raison d'etre*. In this type of environment, staff have little desire to help each other, and leaders view their position primarily as a vehicle for personal achievement. Leaders who allow this to occur find that organizational goals are ignored and that leadership teams have members who play harmful games of politics and act selfishly.

MISUSE AND OVERUSE: HOW LIVING BY PERSONAL CONVICTION CAN WORK AGAINST YOU

Although strong convictions can drive leaders and their teams to deliver breakthrough performance, they can also have a serious downside when relied on heavily, leading to one or more of the following patterns.

Overvaluing One's Own Perspective

This can occur if leaders genuinely believe their views are the only correct ones. This pattern is often associated with fervent religious beliefs; however, in reality, such an orientation generally says more about the individuals than the religion they claim to support. In extreme cases, these leaders may regularly make statements such as "I answer only to God" as a means of invoking moral one-upmanship rather than engage meaningfully in the face of conflict.

More frequently, these less effective leaders may say things such as "This is a matter only the board and I would fully understand." Such an inflexible orientation tends to directly interfere with the leader's ability to build and sustain effective working relationships. Regardless of their other talents, such leaders typically find themselves unable to scale many rungs in the corporate ladder. Leaders who place such a high value on their own points of view also often shut off creative input from their team members.

Failing to "Own" One's Perspectives

A more subtle but related challenge stems from the nature of the leadership role as a position of implied authority. Leaders can fall into the trap of viewing their personal convictions as "correct" by virtue of their leadership role—"I'm right because I'm the boss." Such an orientation, while perhaps not overtly hostile to others' perspectives, nonetheless fails to acknowledge and affirm others' views. Leaders that follow this pattern also run the risk of creating a team of all "yes people" and stifling team creativity. Groups led by such leaders rarely venture outside the box and almost never engage in innovative problem solving. In the end, valuable opportunities to develop understanding and trust through the experiences of work may be lost at the expense of higher performance.

Being Overly Moralistic

Moral thinking and judgments become dangerous the moment they enter the interpersonal realm. Internally statements about what one "should" or "must" do may speak of personal conviction, but externally they may come across as moral one-upmanship, chastising, and a holier-than-thou orientation.

Misuse and Overuse: How Living by Personal Conviction Can Work Against You

Overuse of personal conviction yields the following symptoms:

■ Overvaluing one's own perspective
- Leaders view their beliefs as the only correct ones.
- Leaders are unwilling to consider other perspectives, or even to allow others to state their opinions.

■ Failing to "own" one's perspectives
- Leaders consider themselves to be right on virtue of their position.
- Teams are composed of "yes people" who do not challenge the leader or think creatively.

■ Being overly moralistic
- Conviction comes across as a sermon rather than a point of view.
- Nonsupporters of the leader's view are cast as moral lessers.

Leaders who are very hard on themselves often struggle to avoid being just as hard on their direct reports, their peers, or, even worse, their superiors. People in general have a very low tolerance for being implied to be "moral lessers." Leaders do not get to make this mistake of being moralistic many times before it comes back to haunt them.

So why would a leader make this mistake, not once, but over and over again? Because convictions can create a blind spot. When a decision is proposed or an action is taken that runs against what the leader stands for, he can be thrown into a kind of "moral outrage" that prevents him from seeing the appropriate considerations of interpersonal judgment. The leader then does not think about consequences, reactions, or impressions. Instead, the leader is consumed by outrage. He will react defensively and out of concern, but the tone will come across as a sermon or a lecture.

WHAT TO DO TO BETTER LIVE BY PERSONAL CONVICTION

Finding Role Models

As for all of the competencies discussed in this book, you can take two approaches to finding good mentors that will help you live by your personal convictions. The first is to look for people with a strong reputation in this area. Think about the following questions or pose them to well-connected peers:

- Do you know anyone who really lives by her principles?
- If you had a moral dilemma at work and wanted to talk to a mentor about it, who is the first person you would want to call?
- Who is the best person at supporting his or her convictions without coming across like a preacher?

The second approach is to look for people whose occupation requires them to master this competency to succeed. Faith-based organizations are an excellent place to find people with a strong sense of living by their convictions. Alternatively, persons "of the cloth" who have become effective leaders in secular organizations likely have struggled with balancing their roles and identities and, as such, are good role models. Leaders of organizations that have strong social purposes (e.g., indigent clinics, American Red Cross, American Cancer Society) may also be good mentors.

Additional Opportunities for Personal Development

Strength in personal conviction comes from having a better understanding of yourself and your principles. Participation in organizations that foster a deeper understanding and allegiance with the greater good (e.g., social service organizations, religious groups, other mission-driven associations) can be useful in helping you gain a better understanding of what is most important to you. Another very useful exercise is to conduct a personal inventory of your convictions; Carson Dye's (2000) book, *Leadership in Healthcare: Values at the Top*, provides an approach to use. However, if you need to focus your efforts on a particular deficiency, suggestions for improvement in specific areas are listed below.

Reconnect with Yourself

If you are having problems keeping in touch with your personal convictions, we recommend giving some thought to your "origin story"—the reasons you chose healthcare administration as a profession in the first place. You might even consider digging up the essay you wrote for admission to graduate school, or think back to the first health administration role you took. Spending the time to reconnect with what first brought you into healthcare can help you become a personally stronger, more authentic leader to others.

Find time to think reflectively about your work. You might try scheduling this time at the end of the day, the end of the week, or on an as-needed basis, depending on the challenges you face. Regardless of the frequency, time to reflect, alone or with a trusted colleague or loved one, can be very helpful in remaining in touch with your personal convictions.

Broaden Your Horizons

A powerful way to gain a sense of your personal conviction is to spend time in a context that is foreign to you. When we look into the histories of breakthrough leaders, we notice that many have lived, at some point in their lives, within a culture very different from their own. This experience can help leaders cultivate a far richer understanding of themselves because it enables them to come into regular contact with their own convictions.

Travel is a great way to broaden one's perspective; however, if this is not a realistic option for you, consider reaching out to individuals or groups who hold very different worldviews. If you can think of a group you "just can't understand," they are probably an ideal choice. Outreach can take many forms: visiting a religious gathering, attending a social meeting, or simply sharing dinner conversation. The dialog might focus on how your companion views recent events as related to his beliefs, or how those beliefs have shaped his decisions.

Challenge Your Perspectives

Challenge yourself to fully hear the points of view that most challenge your own by seeking out these perspectives and deeply listening to them. A good exercise involves placing yourself in situations where your only goal is to be more open to others' opinions—for example, by visiting another religion's place of worship or the rally of a competing political party. Learn to recognize within yourself when you begin to close down to the opinions of others or to react with hostility. Chapter 6, "Listening Like You Mean it," provides additional useful guidelines on improving your receptivity to others' ideas.

If you need to become more open-minded about other opinions and perspectives, take it upon yourself to proactively challenge your own perspectives in settings other than the workplace, where it is safer to do so. Have dialogs with people who hold very different views from your own, and challenge yourself to summarize their perspectives aloud before jumping in with rebuttals. Make it a point to find opportunities to give others' perspectives center stage once in a while. You might also work on catching yourself when you want to say, "Do it because I said so." If you do say this, challenge yourself to come up with a clearer rationale for the requested course of action.

Focus Less on Your Personal Goals

If others describe you as focusing too much on your own goals, we recommend you take this feedback seriously. You may be creating a counterproductive work climate—no one will go the extra mile for leaders they see as "out just for themselves." Start by taking an honest look at your motives. What do you hope your achievements will do for you? What will be "enough," and what does "enough" look like? Leaders who are able to confront these questions can start themselves down the road toward a healthier and more rewarding sense of personal conviction.

REFERENCE

Dye, C. 2000. *Leadership in Healthcare: Values at the Top*. Chicago: Health Administration Press.

CHAPTER TWO

Possessing Emotional Intelligence

Two vice presidents at a large health system had the following conversation.

"Karen just knows how to read people and has a real way with them. She really manages herself with poise. She is so different from Rodney. He thinks he is a master motivator, but everyone is afraid of him. His outbursts have gotten worse since he was promoted last year. Who knew he could be such a hothead? He doesn't care about anyone but himself. I know he is smart and has done some great things for our health system, but he is just too wrapped up in himself."

"I think Karen should have gotten the promotion, but she has taken it well. I thought she would leave the health system after being passed over, but she has hung in there. I bet that if Rodney leaves, they will move her up to replace him in an instant. She may not be as creative or smart as Rodney, but she would get better results. I would go to the wall for her."

A year after this conversation took place, the system's board and CEO asked Rodney to leave the health system because he had not been able to garner support for his changes. Karen was immediately moved into the position, much to the elation of the senior leaders of the organization.

This vignette describes a script we frequently see in leadership roles: Drive and skills are enough to earn a promotion but not enough to keep it. Long-term effectiveness depends on the quality of the leader's working relationships, which are in turn a function of the leader's capacity to understand and work effectively with emotions—of others as well as themselves.

WHAT IS POSSESSING EMOTIONAL INTELLIGENCE, AND WHY IS IT IMPORTANT?

Emotional intelligence is a construct that unifies a slate of interpersonal skills. It was first articulated by researchers Salovey and Mayer (1990) and later popularized by author Goleman (1995). Some suggest possessing emotional intelligence is merely having interpersonal skills. However, we believe interpersonal skills are a subset of the broad concept of emotional intelligence. Understanding and working with other people's emotions while understanding and managing your own emotional responses requires emotional intelligence. The most effective leaders have a deeper understanding of their emotions.

> Possessing emotional intelligence means you recognize personal strengths and weaknesses; see the linkages between feelings and behaviors; manage impulsive feelings and distressing emotions; are attentive to emotional cues; show sensitivity and respect for others; challenge bias and intolerance; collaborate and share; are an open communicator; and can handle conflict, difficult people, and tense situations effectively. Emotional intelligence may often be labeled EQ, or emotional intelligence quotient.

WHEN HIGHLY EFFECTIVE LEADERS POSSESS EMOTIONAL INTELLIGENCE

Highly effective leaders regularly find themselves in circumstances where emotions run hot. An emotional charge can be a productive energy source, and emotional intelligence can spell the difference between putting this energy to good use and watching it burn out of control. We can conceptualize these circumstances in terms of the polarities we all face in leadership roles. In each polarity, the optimal approach will involve a balance. Our effectiveness in achieving that balance will be determined by the combination of two forces: (1) our natural orientation toward others and (2) our ability to tweak that orientation. This combination is sometimes called our *emotional quotient* (EQ). Highly effective leaders tend to achieve the most optimal balance between leadership's most critical polarities, a few of which are briefly described below.

Acting with Self-Interest Versus Acting with Selfless Interest

A fundamental polarity in leadership involves the balance between self-interest (what you do to serve your own needs) and selfless interest (what you do to serve the needs of others or the needs of the organization). Balance means both sets of needs are adequately served. If there is too much emphasis on the selfish side, your influence in the organization may erode or fail to develop in the first place. If there is too much emphasis on the selfless side, the responsibilities of your role will erode your familial relationships, health, and well-being.

Most leaders have vulnerabilities, or blind spots, on either side of the balance. On the selfish side, we have the temptations associated with leadership roles. As you reach higher levels, your ability to influence the resources you receive, even your own salary, expands, and the line between purposeful influence and influence for influence's sake becomes difficult to see. Others, such as your direct reports, will feel greater pressure to curry your favor and to convince you that everything is going great (regardless of how things are really going). The selfish temptation is to lose your objectivity and begin "believing your own press releases."

However, there is danger on the selfless side, too. As your influence and resources increase with higher level positions, you will be approached with greater frequency to contribute to causes of all types. You will have expanded opportunities to do good on behalf of your organization and to support pet causes, which may or may not align with your organization's goals. A soft spot can quickly become an Achilles' heel.

This is where cultivating self-awareness comes in. Effective leaders use their self-awareness to identify and overcome their blind spots, enabling them to keep an objective, optimal balance.

Engaging Others Versus Maintaining Distance

It is very difficult for the CEO or other leader to be "one of the gang." Leaders must master a balance between engaging the people they work with and maintaining a distance from them. A healthy balance involves a combination of the two.

An imbalance on either side of this continuum diminishes the leader's effectiveness. If there is too much distance, coworkers will find it difficult to trust you. A lack of engagement with direct reports can create an emotionally cold environment that people do not look forward to coming to and are anxious to leave at the end of the day. Without getting occasional messages of approval, some direct reports will suspect the worst and assume the distance is a signal of personal vulnerability.

For all the danger inherent in failing to engage with coworkers, there is also a danger in overengaging. For some leaders, work relationships serve emotional needs that are above and beyond the accomplishment of work-related goals. If leaders find they need regular approval from the people they work with, they may be too quick to give in to requests from direct reports or, alternatively, may shamelessly gratify their bosses. Another common pattern is possessiveness around working relationships, in which leaders not only fail to facilitate but actively block the development of social networks that do not pass through them.

Exceptional leaders exhibit enough engagement that relationships of trust, familiarity, and comfort can evolve. On the other hand, they keep enough distance that these leaders can pursue with some objectivity the kinds of candid feedback, appraisals, and personnel changes that may be in the best interests of the organization's goals.

Trusting in Self Versus Trusting in Others

Trust forms another polarity requiring careful balance. Leaders who are too trusting will overdelegate responsibilities, handing them to others and putting them entirely out of their mind. If the work does not get done or does not get done properly, they will be quick to pass along blame and will have trouble recognizing their own failure to provide a supportive check-in.

On the flipside are leaders who place too much trust in themselves and not enough in others. This is the more common pattern of suboptimal performance, perhaps in part because it tends to get leaders in less immediate trouble than the former pattern. Leaders who do not learn to place adequate trust in others will either fail to delegate, creating a growth-stifling work environment in which no high-potential employee will stay for long, or underdelegate, giving tasks to others but then checking in so frequently and with such force that the tasks take twice the work.

Highly effective leaders achieve optimal balance of trust by delegating important aspects of work to others while continuing to monitor that work in ways that are respectful and nonintrusive.

WHEN POSSESSING EMOTIONAL INTELLIGENCE IS NOT ALL IT COULD BE

Less effective leaders do not use the full extent of their emotional intelligence. Ways in which they fall short of accomplishing this competency involve the following.

Lacking Concern for Others

At times, leaders may lack an appropriate level of concern for others. They may get so wrapped up in working toward the organizational mission that they fail to recognize the individual needs of others around them. At other times, leaders may simply be so self-absorbed that they fundamentally have no respect for others.

Needing Approval

Some leaders are overly concerned with how they are perceived by others. Their need for approval prevents their personal conviction from driving their principles and actions. A common example is found in CEOs who are very confident and self-assured until they get in front of their boards, where they will quickly back down if challenged. Other common examples include leaders who are so concerned with being popular that they are unwilling to make tough decisions that might offend some of their team members. These leaders are sometimes called "country-club managers."

Being Volatile

Leaders who are passionate about their jobs will occasionally be upset—maybe very upset—by the decisions or actions of others that frustrate their goals. Strength in leadership comes not from stifling these emotions but rather from controlling them. Leaders are described as volatile if others cannot predict what will set them off or if their emotions seem to control them.

Mistrusting Others

Highly effective leaders who have a strong grasp of emotional intelligence are willing to trust others. They delegate often and regularly and help others develop. They share both responsibility and accountability. It is rarely said of them that they have to check everything before anything is done. Leaders should work hard to communicate the big picture and learn how to empower others.

> ## When Possessing Emotional Intelligence Is Not All It Could Be
>
> When emotional intelligence is not as strong as it could be, a leader may be described in the following ways:
>
> - Lacking concern for others
>   - Individual needs of others are not recognized.
>   - Self-absorption prevents the leader from respecting others.
> - Needing approval
>   - Approval rather than personal conviction drives action.
> - Being volatile
>   - Staff cannot predict what will set off their leader.
>   - Emotions are in control of the leader rather than the leader being in control of his or her emotions.
> - Mistrusting others
>   - Everything has to go through the leader before anything can get done.
>   - Work is not delegated, and staff is not empowered.

MISUSE AND OVERUSE: HOW POSSESSING EMOTIONAL INTELLIGENCE CAN WORK AGAINST YOU

Can you be too emotionally intelligent? Perhaps not. However, emotional intelligence definitely can be misapplied and at the expense of higher performance in the following ways.

Getting by on One's Good Graces

Emotional intelligence tends to be highly prized in senior leadership roles; all else being equal, leaders with higher EQs (emotional intelligence quotient) will be more favored for promotion or, in the case of downsizing, more likely to be retained. We all share a bias to want to work with colleagues who are agreeable, and no one knows how to be agreeable better than a high-EQ leader.

Conversely, high-EQ leaders are also most adept at making a case to overlook their underperformance. High-EQ leaders can be less effective in other areas and will suffer fewer confrontations about it. They tend to have political networks that are far stronger than that of their peers and can tap them for support whenever poor performance becomes a concern. Some leaders hold on to senior roles for long periods through little more than their good graces and social ties.

Overextending the Emotional Role

Occasionally, leaders with high EQs may enjoy the emotional aspects of their work to the point that they may actually foster a volatile work environment. The patterns of emotional crisis and then working through and repairing relationships may be familiar to the point of providing greater comfort than a more stable environment would. However, needlessly volatile environments unnecessarily draw attention away from the pursuit of organizational goals.

For some leaders, serving as on-call negotiators or interpersonal problem solvers can be gratifying roles. These leaders may be reluctant to let others work challenges out for themselves or, in the case of direct reports, work with them to develop their own emotional intelligence.

Avoiding Noninterpersonal Aspects of Work

Some high-EQ leaders focus too much time on the interpersonal aspects of their roles. These parts of their roles are where they get the most positive feedback, but they may not be adding the most value. For example, more time than necessary may be taken up maintaining work ties (e.g., always finding the time for every social event) or processing interpersonal exchanges that may not need the level of scrutiny they receive, when the time would be better spent addressing other critical elements of the leader's role (e.g., budgeting, planning).

WHAT TO DO TO DEVELOP BETTER EMOTIONAL INTELLIGENCE

Finding Role Models

High-EQ leaders tend to be found in the greatest numbers in human resources, pastoral care, counseling, or social service roles. In these roles a higher EQ is required for effectiveness than in most other positions, opportunities to develop and hone these skills are more frequent, and the skill set is tested more routinely. Whatever the challenges you face in your working environment, chances are people in these types of roles have seen it and worse. (A caveat: not *all* such individuals have a high EQ; the notes about overuse earlier in the chapter also apply to individuals in these groups. Be sure a potential mentor has a reputation for having a high EQ.)

Additional Opportunities for Personal Development

While there are many books, seminars, and courses on this topic, the best way to improve your EQ is to improve the quality of the feedback you receive about yourself and your relationships. The opposite of self-awareness is blind spots, and we all have them to a greater or lesser degree. The only way to surface these blind spots is to receive feedback about them and to be willing to internalize what that feedback means.

You can improve the quality of the feedback you receive in a variety of ways:

- Develop more structured ways of getting feedback (e.g., use 360-degree programs, ask subordinates to provide input to third parties about how they feel about you).
- Improve your ability to "hear" feedback (e.g., work with a facilitator or a coach).

Figure 2.1. Johari Window

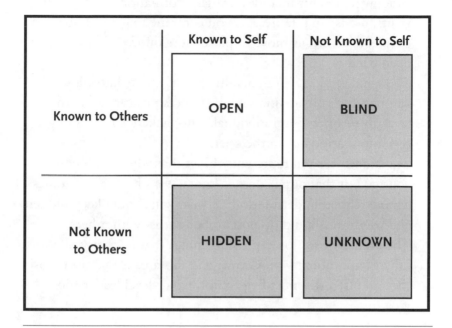

- Create a climate more conducive to feedback (e.g., conduct staff training or build feedback reviews into the ongoing work that you do).

A final suggestion that has been used in the literature on this topic for some time is the Johari Window (see Figure 2.1), which is discussed in some detail in *Leadership in Healthcare: Values at the Top* (Dye 2000). This concept helps leaders better identify blind spots and develop ways to address them.

The Johari Window, which was named after the first names of its inventors, Joseph Luft and Harry Ingham from Westinghouse, describes the process of human interaction. A four-paned "window" divides awareness into four quadrants: open, hidden, blind, and unknown. The lines dividing the four panes can move as awareness changes. The four quadrants represent the following:

- The open section represents things that you know about yourself and that others know about you. The knowledge that this window represents includes factual information, feelings, wants, needs, and desires. As you continue to get to know people, the sections move to place more information into the open window.
- The blind section represents things that others know about you but that you are unaware of. Blind spots can affect the level of trust between individuals; the challenge here is to get this information out in the open.
- The hidden section represents things that you know about yourself but that others do not know. With higher EQ comes a more refined understanding of what you should keep hidden and what you should disclose to build trust with others.
- The unknown section represents things that neither you nor others know about you. Growing in this area is the most sensitive but often the most helpful for higher-level leadership growth.

REFERENCES

Dye, C. 2000. *Leadership in Healthcare: Values at the Top.* Chicago: Health Administration Press.

Goleman, D. 1995. *Emotional Intelligence: Why It Can Matter More Than IQ.* New York: Bantam.

Salovey, P., and J. D. Mayer. 1990. "Emotional Intelligence." *Imagination, Cognition, and Personality* 9: 185–211.

CORNERSTONE 2

Compelling
Vision

CHAPTER THREE

Being Visionary

Crisis. Jill, the CEO of East Main Hospital, lay awake Wednesday night, still thinking through the board meeting she attended earlier that day. While she had maintained good relations with the board during the first year in her role, the "honeymoon" definitely appeared to be ending. East Main seemed to be suffering setback after setback. The main hospital, a historic building, cost more and more to keep up to code every year. The inner city itself was in the throes of a major economic downturn, and it was getting harder and harder to compete with the suburban hospitals for healthcare personnel. Physicians had the run of the place; healthcare capital equipment was driven almost entirely by efforts to recruit and retain physicians. Every day it seemed like her attention was being divided into smaller and smaller chunks.

Complacency. As the new CEO of Metro West Hospital (MWH), Jack finally felt that he had "arrived." Recently promoted from the COO role, he was following in the footsteps of Brad, who retired earlier in the year after running the hospital for over a decade. Brad had himself been hired from the COO role and had brought with him a deep knowledge of the hospital's operations. During his tenure, Brad had made this solid community hospital even more efficient. Profitability was strong, turnover was low, staff were highly satisfied, and physicians were loyal and high quality. MWH had little competition in their market, an affluent suburb of a medium-sized Midwestern city. The biggest challenge Jack saw in the coming years was planning for increased capacity as the suburbs continued to grow.

These two scenarios both offer opportunities for a leader to develop and articulate a compelling vision, although both present formidable challenges to doing so. Jill's situation is perhaps more familiar in healthcare these days: routine, dramatic changes so numerous that they become difficult to keep track of, let alone address. Jill's challenge is to draw people's attention away from the crises they individually face long enough to allow them to see a collective vision—a beacon of hope concerning how the organization could be in the future.

Jack's hospital, in contrast, may at first glance seem to be almost on autopilot. But while chaos is a more readily apparent barrier to higher performance, complacency can be as much of a barrier, if not more so. How do you motivate a group that is already feeling comfortable to take their organization even further?

WHAT IS BEING VISIONARY, AND WHY IS IT IMPORTANT?

Being visionary means that you see the future clearly, anticipate large-scale and local changes that will affect the organization and its environment, are able to project the organization into the future and envision multiple potential scenarios/outcomes, have a broad way of looking at trends, and are able to design competitive strategies and plans based on future possibilities.

In our experience, *vision* is one of most sought after competencies at the top levels of leadership. Vision can be most straightforwardly defined as the capacity to create effective plans for your organization's future based on a clear understanding of trends, uncertainties, risks, and rewards. Some might call it the art of developing strategy. Highly effective leaders who have strength of vision will position their organizations to take advantage of the trends they are discerning. For example, in healthcare, visionary leaders may see new clinical and technological advances long before they are prevalent and may commit their organizations to adopt them as they become available. They may see opportunities to get physicians more committed to their organizations by linking these physicians through more cutting-edge practices. We contrast this with the "chasing-the-trends" herd mentality; exceptional leaders have the capacity to identify the trends that make sense strategically and to adopt them early, before others copy them.

Organizations who have visionary leaders tend to be more successful. They are usually the first to market with new ideas and technology; as a result, they often have better profitability, which allows them to attract higher-quality physicians and, ultimately, better serve their communities.

WHEN HIGHLY EFFECTIVE LEADERS ARE VISIONARY

Although visioning is best thought of as an ongoing process, there is a definable sequence associated with that process. The quality of vision relies on a solid awareness and understanding of broad trends and their implications. From these, a vision slowly takes shape, tempered (but not stifled) by the critical thinking of the key people needed to pursue it and communicated to those needed to implement it. Highly effective leaders use necessary skills to accomplish each of these elements of the visioning process.

Having an Awareness of Trends

Many, perhaps most, senior leaders have mastered the ability to track important trends in healthcare. If we go into any leader's office, chances are we will see copies of publications such as *Modern Healthcare, Healthcare Executive*, and possibly several trade journals more specific to their functional areas. We may even hear about news updates on the various health administration listservs. These are good resources for keeping track of trends within healthcare, but none give a complete picture of the major trends happening outside the industry that will affect healthcare. These publications also tend to be "preprocessed"—the conclusions have already been drawn for the reader.

Exceptional leaders dig deeper to better understand the emerging trends. They are also broader thinkers who follow developments that are often outside of healthcare. If asked what they are reading from outside of the healthcare industry, good leaders may cite the occasional business publication. Visionary leaders, on the other hand, are more likely to cite multiple sources with compelling, though perhaps indirect, associations with their leadership and industry roles, including biographies of successful leaders throughout history, analyses of broad economic trends (such as the effects of energy policy on productivity), books on urban planning and development, articles on sustainable communities, or analyses of the rise and fall of ancient societies.

For exceptional leaders, this pattern extends far beyond what they read. Imagine for a moment that you wanted to learn more about how nanotechnology may affect health services delivery in the future. If you were a typical leader, you might scour the health administration journals to examine the implications others are drawing about likely outcomes. Or you might go further and review non-healthcare periodicals such as *MIT Technology Review*, *The Economist*, or even *Wired*. But if you were a truly visionary leader who sought to move your organization to the frontier, you could go as far as developing contacts and links well outside the field, particularly with the advent of the Internet. Many scholars maintain lists of individuals who have requested updates on what is coming out of their labs. These lists contain other scholars but also often contain industry members who simply want to stay informed about trends that could affect their businesses. They may even reach out to venture capitalists who are on the forefront of developing innovations.

Understanding Risks, Rewards, and Uncertainties

Analyses to support strategic decision making represent something of a paradox. On the one hand, a fact-based analysis is essential to sound judgment, offering leaders their only hope to develop an even marginally objective understanding of what the future holds. However, decisions always involve an emotional as well as a rational element; risk and uncertainty are always interpreted subjectively as well as objectively. Regardless of how well-reasoned a course of action sounds, there will be resistance stemming from the unfamiliarity the direction represents. People would prefer to believe that change is unnecessary; an exceptional leader's vision is strong enough to allow their trust in your leadership to overcome that tendency.

Communicating Vision

If the process is worked through effectively, the vision becomes the logical conclusion—the clear answer to the question raised by the analysis. There may be anxiety about how to get there, but there should be clarity about the appropriateness of the vision for the organization.

We will discuss more about turning the vision into words and words into actions in the next chapter. For now, we will leave it at the following key distinction: A good vision describes how the *organization* will be a better place because of the work of its people, but a breakthrough vision describes how the *world* will be a better place because of the work of the organization.

WHEN BEING VISIONARY IS NOT ALL IT COULD BE

We mentioned that strategic vision is one of the qualities that all boards look for in their senior hires. This competency, more so than the others in this cluster, tends to be the "rare bird." In other words, there are far more senior leaders with excellent trust building skills, outstanding communication skills, or both than there are strategic visionaries.

Part of the shortfall may be cognitive in nature; some elements of the visioning competency are apparently very difficult to develop. However, less effective leaders may also make the following mistakes.

Focusing Too Much on Tactical Operations

Many executives work long and hard hours day after day but seem to have no long-term impact on their organizations or communities. They become so mired in the tactical, routine matters that they do not have the time to evaluate and develop long-term strategies.

Leaders who lack vision are often relegated to what many call "putting out daily fires." One well-known CEO said, "The best leaders are those who have the ability to transcend the day-to-day and see out into the future. Those are the leaders who are going to shape needed change in our field." In some management circles, this is referred to as being proactive rather than reactive.

For some leaders, promotion into a role that allows for broader and more long-range influence provides a welcome opportunity to think strategically. For others, however, the opportunity is either not taken or is not taken far enough. Sometimes the reason is discomfort or the feeling that reaching out is too much like "sticking one's neck out." For other leaders, the capacity to think strategically has yet to be developed.

Other leaders have the capacity to develop strategic vision, but the comfort of their operation's focus or their lack of experience with the visioning process, or both, hold them back. Healthcare tends to provide many opportunities to focus on day-to-day challenges if leaders decide to do so at the expense of building and communicating a compelling vision.

For those leaders who do manage to focus some time and energy on thinking about the future, there is the risk that the vision will remain nothing more than an idea that is discussed from time to time during social conversation or perhaps just once in a true operational context. In other words, the vision may be presented but not meaningfully hardwired into operational meetings.

Restricting Focus to Healthcare

Another way in which vision can fall short of the ceiling is if leaders focus their sights strictly on the business of their hospitals. Within health administration, already a high-involvement profession, there is a tendency to become cloistered. The risk here is of losing sight of how healthcare is affected by broader trends, as well as how healthcare can affect well-being above and beyond the service lines the hospital counts on for revenue.

When Being Visionary Is Not All It Could Be

When vision is lacking, it can look like any of the following:

- Focusing too much on tactical operations
  - Control of day-to-day "fires" take precedence over long-range planning.
  - Long-term perspectives are not structured into regular operations.

- Restricting focus to healthcare
  - Social and professional networks and information sources reside almost entirely within the healthcare industry.
  - There is little intellectual curiosity about broader trends or changes.

- Relying on external counsel
  - The analytic work of others is heavily relied on, and conclusions are not questioned.
  - The organization follows the leader and does whatever the other hospitals are doing, with inadequate analysis as to whether it is appropriate.

- Undervaluing divergent perspectives
  - Staff go along with a vision simply because they want to stay on the leader's good side.
  - Concerns and ideas about the future are not discussed.

Relying on External Counsel

The sheer complexity of health administration creates a need for help in putting all the pieces together. Information digests, consultants, and other sources can be immensely helpful here, as long as leaders maintain a healthy skepticism. Questioning takes time, focus, and energy—it is tempting to let it fall by the wayside (analytic help is what you are paying for in the first place, right?).

A similar pattern we see frequently is "following the leader," where a hospital or group of hospitals are known for being early adopters of trends and thus become the de facto leaders for the broader industry. There is some psychological safety in deferring judgment to well-regarded, well-run hospitals. Sometimes, perhaps often, the strategy works. But there is little in this strategy that would suggest breakthrough leadership by an administrator.

Undervaluing Divergent Perspectives

Strategic vision can also fall short if it is too tightly ascribed to a single leader—something that happens when leaders fail to engage their teams in honing, evolving, and challenging their organizational visions. For leaders who possess adequate power, peers and direct reports will go along with a vision they do not believe in simply to stay on the leader's good side, and they are not encouraged to discuss their concerns or ideas about the future. The energy they bring to the effort is thus borrowed energy, which is soon depleted and in need of a refill.

We can extend this example to other situations in which leaders resist challenges to their visions or resist the visioning process entirely. Some leaders view the visioning process as frivolous; they pride themselves in their abilities to address problems in the moment or in chasing opportunities in whatever form they may take. The approach may provide them the greatest comfort, but it will not get the level of commitment from their needed collaborators that a shared vision will deliver. This is in large part the point Jim Collins (2001) makes in distinguishing "foxes" from "hedgehogs" in his book, *Good to Great*. In this book, the hedgehogs take a complex world and simplify it, while the foxes are scattered and try out many different strategies at the same time.

MISUSE AND OVERUSE: HOW BEING VISIONARY CAN WORK AGAINST YOU

Without a doubt, leaders can focus too much on vision to the detriment of their organizations. When these downsides appear, it is often attributable to either an imbalance somewhere within the visioning process or overzealousness about visioning in and of itself.

Balancing Poorly Between Operations and Planning

Leaders can become so engaged with the visioning process that the day-to-day management of the enterprise is ignored. There needs to be a proper balance between long-term strategic focus and short-term tactics. Problems often occur when leaders place too much emphasis on business development, strategic planning, and cutting deals. In the excitement of pushing new and exciting initiatives forward, operations may receive diminished focus, and the executives running operations may feel like second-class citizens. The imbalance can create a host of implementation problems as well. Planning executives may not develop the level of understanding of operations necessary to forge realistic plans. Conversely, operations executives may not have the influence they should on the strategic planning process, resulting in less buy-in and engagement with its implementation.

Focusing Too Much on the Planning Process

Another symptom of overzealous planning is a fondness for process over outcome. Leaders with this pattern are overly eager to try out a variety of strategic planning approaches to "see where it takes us." Moving through the planning process becomes the end in and of itself. This results in an inordinate amount of time

Misuse and Overuse: How Being Visionary Can Work Against You

If a person overuses this competency, it can result in the following problems:

- Balancing poorly between operations and planning
  - Business development and strategic planning executives are elevated above the key operations people.
  - Day-to-day operations are ignored.
- Focusing too much on the planning process
  - Technique is valued over substance.
  - Data are collected far beyond the point of diminishing returns.
  - Execution is unnecessarily slowed down.
- Overemphasizing implementation
  - New plans are created too frequently, and old plans are abandoned with inadequate (or inadequately communicated) rationale.
  - Colleagues develop attitudes of "waiting it out."

moving through elaborate strategic planning retreats and a multitude of three-ring binders full of objectives, most of which are never achieved.

Another type of overzealous focus shows up in the use of data. Healthcare has more data sets available for analysis than almost any other industry; it can be very tempting to believe more is more to the point that analyses are pursued far beyond the point of diminishing returns. Executive teams can quickly fall into the bad habit of allowing analysis to unnecessarily slow down the execution of new initiatives or the implementation of needed changes.

Overemphasizing Implementation

To paraphrase Thomas Edison, genius involves one part inspiration and 99 parts perspiration. Indeed, some leaders are so effective in crafting truly compelling visions that they overemphasize the vision itself at the expense of its implementation. Little attention may be paid to how the vision will be translated into specific plans. Worse, new visions may be created before they are needed and before the old visions have either proved obsolete or have been given a reasonable chance to take hold. In these cases, colleagues in the hospital may quickly develop an attitude of "let's just wait this one out," and trust on both sides will suffer in the process. (See Chapter 4, "Communicating Vision," and Chapter 14, "Driving Results," for more ideas about improving your implementation focus.)

WHAT TO DO TO BECOME A BETTER VISIONARY

Finding Role Models

If you are at a below-C level position, you may find useful guidance from senior leaders, as well as from leaders within the business development and marketing departments of your organization. At higher levels, however, identifying good mentors for vision can be very challenging, and you will likely need to look outside your own organization to find them. In thinking about who might have real strength in this area, ask yourself the following questions:

- Where are the innovations happening in healthcare right now?
- Where are the success stories?
- Where has a health system been taken from "good to great?"

You may need to develop relationships with consultants who are well traveled and well versed on new trends and ideas. Ongoing networking with healthcare peers outside your market can also be helpful.

Additional Opportunities for Personal Development

A very effective way to become more visionary is to expand your horizons beyond healthcare. Make sure you have opportunities for the outside world to reach you. Be mindful of the continuous tendency for healthcare to creep into the social engagements you keep and the books on your nightstand; set aside some time and focus specifically on non-healthcare issues. Ensure time is allocated to interact with leaders from other industries. Finally, be certain that ample time is spent involved in community activities.

In terms of conceptualizing strategic options, the classic text is Michael Porter's (1998) *Competitive Strategy: Techniques for Analyzing Industries and Competitors*. If your education included a course in strategy, chances are either this text was assigned or the text that you did use quoted liberally from it. The conceptual models in this text will be familiar to almost anyone with a degree in business or administration; make reading this one a top priority.

For the actual process of developing a vision, we recommend *Visionary Leadership* by Burt Nanus (1992). It is a very readable guide to what a vision statement needs to do and how it needs to be created to accomplish its goals. Although the examples used in Nanus's book are becoming dated, the methods are not.

Finally, for a healthcare-specific look at strategy development, we recommend *Healthcare Strategy: In Pursuit of Competitive Advantage* by Roice Luke, Stephen Walston, and Patrick Plummer (2003).

REFERENCES

Collins, J. 2001. *Good to Great: Why Some Companies Make the Leap...And Others Don't*. New York: Harper Business.

Porter, M. 1998. *Competitive Strategy: Techniques for Analyzing Industries and Competitors*. New York: Free Press.

Nanus, B. 1992. *Visionary Leadership*. San Francisco: Jossey-Bass.

Luke, R. D., S. L. Walston, and P. M. Plummer. 2003. *Healthcare Strategy: In Pursuit of Competitive Advantage*. Chicago: Health Administration Press.

CHAPTER FOUR

Communicating Vision

Maria had just been appointed CEO, her first time holding the title. She was ecstatic but humbled. She had been in the organization for the past five years, and, as the senior business development person, had led the development of Vision 2020, the organization's long-range strategic plan. Vision 2020 incorporated a $300 million rebuilding and renovation program, an outreach program, a significantly advanced clinical information system, and a new quality initiative that could truly create the "health system of the future." While the financial challenges to fund this project were enormous, even greater in Maria's mind was the essential requirement that the entire physician and employee community be totally engaged in the change initiative.

Maria had discussed this challenge with her executive coach, who suggested that she think about the linkage between change and communication. She began her weekend with the goal of developing a set of outlines that would captivate the physicians and employees when she started her "town hall" meetings next month.

This vignette goes to the heart of the implementation of vision. Leaders must engage various stakeholders to make them understand the rationale for change; leaders must, in essence, create a compelling call to action. To illustrate this point, consider this statement based on Greek history: When Pericles spoke, people said, "how well he speaks." But when Demosthenes spoke, they said, "let us march."

In the previous chapter, we discussed what it means to be visionary. Developing and using vision as an instrument of organizational change requires effective communication of that vision—turning a set of strategic and often complex concepts into a compelling "story" of where the organization is, where it will go, and how it is going to get there.

We call this competency *communicating vision* for several reasons. First, we want to distinguish it from the more general concept of communication, which begins to equate with leadership itself when defined broadly. In this chapter, we specifically address how highly effective leaders communicate vision, and how they create an environment where staff and physicians feel compelled to move with them toward that vision.

WHAT IS COMMUNICATING VISION, AND WHY IS IT IMPORTANT?

Communicating vision throughout any change process is essential to its success. At the same time, it is also incredibly challenging to effectively pull off. Most leaders routinely underestimate the amount of communication necessary to drive change efforts; as a result, many employees inevitably feel lost and confused in the change process and may stick even more closely to their old but familiar habits.

> **Communicating vision** means that you distill complex strategies into a compelling call to march, inspire and help others see a core reason for the organization to make change, talk beyond the day-to-day tactical matters that face the organization, show confidence and optimism about the future state of the organization, and engage others to join in.

Effective leaders not only communicate about day-to-day issues but also about vision. In his book *Leading Change*, noted scholar John Kotter (1996) describes the level of vision-related communication in comparison to total workplace communication during a change effort. In his estimation, vision-related communication tends to comprise only about half of 1 percent of the communication people receive about their work. With this much competition, communication had *better* be captivating!

Spending time communicating future vision also helps ensure that "everyone is on the same page." It aids in collaboration and enhances the coordination of work effort.

WHEN HIGHLY EFFECTIVE LEADERS COMMUNICATE VISION

Although there are as many communication styles as there are communicators, several qualities make any communication style stronger. Keep these in mind, and your communication will begin to reflect them.

Communicating Clearly

Discussing clarity in vision communication may appear trite—after all, who would argue *against* communication clarity? However, in reality, few among us are as clear as we could be, as frequently as we could be, though most of us would like to think otherwise.

Let us compare communicating vision to marketing. Think about the marketing slogans that you have found most memorable. What did they have in common? Chances are they were straightforward, novel, even catchy—and without a single vague or unnecessary word. If they were really good, they stuck in your mind—you could not help but think of them. These same structural elements can be usefully applied to vision communication. You want these ideas to be compelling and to stick in people's minds.

Communicating Widely

Effective leaders ensure that everyone who will be responsible for moving the vision forward hear it. They also use a multitude of communication methods to describe vision so that the message fully permeates. This is an area that separates exceptional leaders from their well-intentioned but less-effective counterparts. Because communication can be labor intensive, shortcuts become tempting. A handy example is placing a message in the corporate newsletter and considering the communication finished. Such a step may make sense if there is an explicit expectation on the part of all staff that they read the newsletter *and* if the step is effectively monitored, but it is hard to justify otherwise.

Highly effective leaders will take the communication process even farther. Beyond simply ensuring the message is heard, they will ensure that the message is *discussed*. For example, they might instruct managers to explicitly incorporate a discussion of the vision into their next staff meeting and report back on what was discussed.

WHEN COMMUNICATING VISION IS NOT ALL IT COULD BE

When communication falls short of captivating, often one or more of the following may be the reason.

Lacking Clarity, Focus, or Information

Clarity can suffer from a number of problems. The communication may lack clarity because the vision itself lacks clarity. Alternatively, the communication may lack focus; it may contain too many elements for people to easily wrap their heads around. Still another problem stems from communicating too little information about the how of the vision. The further the vision is from the current state of affairs, the greater the need for some indication of the path to getting there. Without this path, staff may dismiss the vision as being out of hand—a risk made far more likely if there is recent history of abandoned visions.

Lacking Meaning for the Audience

The challenge of making a broad organizational vision meaningful at department and subdepartment levels is usually beyond the capa-

When Communicating Vision Is Not All It Could Be

Communication in the realm of strategic vision will often fall short for any of the following reasons:

- Lacking clarity, focus, or information
  - A visual picture is not created either because it is unclear or it contains too many elements.
  - Lack of thought about the how makes the vision sound far-fetched.
- Lacking meaning for the audience
  - The importance of individual roles is not adequately addressed.
- Communicating infrequently
  - The vision is rolled out and then rarely referred to again.

bilities of any individual leader. Effective leaders know this and work with managers to develop local interpretations of how the efforts of a given division, department, or team will fit into this broader vision. Without this careful linkage, staff may only receive "the corporate take" on the vision and may have difficulty viewing their roles as part of that vision.

Another frequent problem is the articulation of a vision that does not clearly express how the vision affects everyone, and how everyone affects the vision. This is a risk any time a vision communication places special emphasis on a specific aspect of operations. Common examples include vision statements that draw special attention to the physicians, nurses, profitable service lines, or quality improvement initiatives. If poorly communicated, the vision will leave the counterparts (e.g., non-physicians, non-nurses) feeling excluded.

Communicating Infrequently

Although communication plans can (and should) be designed to be highly efficient, they are still typically time and resource intensive. Communications is a tempting place to cut corners, and so corners are often cut. The best prevention here is to arrange a review of all internal communications coming from the corporate level to ensure they make some mention of future plans. Think about it this way: Any time the vision of the future state of the organization is *not* mentioned, the status quo will take front-stage attention.

MISUSE AND OVERUSE: HOW COMMUNICATING VISION CAN WORK AGAINST YOU

In relation to vision, overcommunication per se is not nearly as frequent as undercommunication. When communication fails, it is usually because of a problem with the communication itself rather than its frequency. The following are patterns that will cause your communication to be ineffective, regardless of frequency.

Communicating Vision as an "End" Rather than a "Means"

Occasionally, leaders may be accused of "talking a great game" and getting people excited about an idea or strategy that they are ultimately unable to implement. They may routinely be caught up in the excitement of thinking (or dreaming) about what the future could be like, but the actions needed to make this future happen are conspicuously absent. The vision is thus discussed as a concept permanently divorced from the present day—a beautiful mirage across the wide chasm of inaction. The danger of this pattern is greatest in groups where no great sense of urgency has been cultivated to overcome the comfort of the status quo.

Misuse and Overuse: How Communicating Vision Can Work Against You

When your communication is ineffective, regardless of frequency, one of the following is most likely the cause:

■ Communicating vision as an "end" rather than a "means"
  • Communication is emphasized at the expense of implementation.
  • Time is spent talking about doing instead of actually doing.

■ Viewing vision as the "program du jour"
  • Motivation building rather than direction setting is the primary goal.
  • Visions change too frequently and are thought of as gimmick programs.

■ Communicating too specifically
  • Setting a timeline for the vision will eventually force the need to develop a new vision.
  • Vision becomes something that can be proved or disproved.

Viewing Vision as the "Program du Jour"

Some leaders do not fully recognize both the power and the responsibility associated with setting and communicating organizational vision. For some, the vision is viewed more trivially and is viewed as a slogan for the occasional staff pep rallies. For others, particularly high-energy leaders who pride themselves for "turning on a dime," the vision may change too rapidly over time, causing confusion and frustration among their staff. Leaders may try out so many different kinds of visions that staff and physicians may view them as just another gimmick program. Healthcare has been known for this, and leaders need to be cautious about falling into this trap.

Communicating Too Specifically

Communications about vision can be too specific in a number of ways. Consider an organization that may develop visions with specific objective goals (e.g., "We will garner 40 percent of the inpatient market share in the area," or "We will be the top provider of heart surgeries by market share in our market"). What if your organization achieves those types of measured goals? Your vision would dissolve, and you would need a new one.

Another example of communicating too specifically relates to timelines. Timelines are terrific for operational goals, but putting a vision on a timeline is often a mistake. Say you set "three years from now" as the time your vision will be achieved. You have just turned the vision into something that can be proved or disproved. People can start to decide early on whether they think the vision will be achieved; if it starts to look undoable, it may be abandoned prematurely. In short, it devolves into an operational goal and loses some of its original power to unite and energize.

WHAT TO DO TO BETTER COMMUNICATE VISION

Finding Role Models

The best way to find mentors in this area is to ask yourself, Who do I find most compelling to listen to? Who paints the most vivid, most exciting, and most believable pictures of the future? Once you have identified these individuals, take note of what they say, how they say it, and what about their communication really reaches you. These individuals need not be people you know personally—for example, politicians and religious leaders are some of the most powerful communicators. What is most important in this exercise is to develop the discipline of attending to the elements that make these communications really work.

Another approach you can take is to identify people (your peers and direct reports, for example) others seem to listen to the most. They need not be leaders you find particularly compelling; sometimes, it can be useful to zero-in on people who surprise you with their ability to captivate others. In these cases, try to learn what it is about this person's communication style that others find so intriguing and look for elements that you can adopt to your advantage.

Additional Opportunities for Personal Development

There are many excellent books available on improving your communication style. For clear and concise writing, the single best source we have seen is *Revising Prose* by Richard Lanham (1999), in any edition. It is a concise, well-written, enjoyable read focusing specifically on clarity and economy of words.

To develop your skills in turning analyses into compelling graphical statements, we highly recommend the works of Edward Tufte. Tufte (2001) has published a series of books on how to present data in captivating ways, including the classic *The Visual Display of Quantitative Information* . He has developed a cult following among some of the more powerful strategic speakers we know. A good place to start is his monograph, *The Cognitive Style of PowerPoint* (Tufte 2003). All are available via online booksellers or through www.edwardtufte.com.

The process of communicating vision in ways that facilitate change are well described in John Kotter's (1996) book, *Leading Change*. This book is widely regarded as a classic on this topic; we highly recommend it.

If you are interested in fine tuning your public speaking skills, there is no better method than practice followed immediately by candid feedback. Because this can often be very difficult to drum up in the workplace, consider a course with the local chapter of Toastmasters International.[1] (If you have no local chapter, consider starting one.) The sole focus of this group is to improve the speaking skills of its members. We are told that the quality of the experience does differ depending on the chapter's membership; however, in general, leaders' and professional speakers' experiences alike have been very favorable with this organization.

NOTE

1. Please visit www.toastmasters.org for more information about this organization.

REFERENCES

Kotter, J. 1996. *Leading Change*. Boston: Harvard Business School Press.

Lanham, R. 1999. *Revising Prose*, 4th ed. New York: Longman.

Tufte, E. 2001. *The Visual Display of Quantitative Information*. Cheshire, CT: Graphics Press.

———. 2003. *The Cognitive Style of PowerPoint*. Cheshire, CT: Graphics Press.

CHAPTER FIVE

Earning Loyalty and Trust

Don was nearing the end of his career and was starting to struggle with it. His tenure as the CEO of a large academic medical center began 15 years ago, during a time of resource plenty. Don had practiced as a general physician with the hospital for decades before entering management. He carried considerable social capital throughout the medical center; his wit, charm, and people skills had served him very well throughout most of his tenure. Most importantly, early in his career as CEO, Don had been able to create and sustain highly compelling visions. People were excited to work with him and follow him. Unlike many other academic centers in the 1980s and 1990s, Don's hospital experienced remarkable success. It recruited world-renowned physicians, grew a vast outreach program, and amassed significant cash reserves. But now Don's rosy view of the world was costing him his credibility. In public forums, he reassured people that things were going well and getting better—a story the business papers regularly refuted and many of his senior executives quietly questioned. The staff of the hospital liked him and wanted to believe him, but they were finding it harder and harder to do so. The fact was that the medical center had lost 10 percent of its market share, no longer had a top-ten transplant program, and had lost several leading clinical researchers. Financial results were also in question, with the organization needing to use cash reserves to cover operating losses. The bottom line is that, despite his vision, Don had lost credibility with his followers.

As this vignette illustrates, having and articulating a vision is not enough to ensure successful development and implementation of that vision. A trust level with stakeholders must be established first.

Success in communicating vision depends strongly on the receptivity of the audience. Receptivity, in turn, is heavily dependent on trust. This chapter is about developing, cultivating, and repairing these relationships of trust as necessary.

WHAT IS EARNING LOYALTY AND TRUST, AND WHY IS IT IMPORTANT?

> **Earning loyalty and trust** means you are a direct and truthful person; are willing to admit mistakes; are sincerely interested in the concerns and dreams of others; show empathy and a generally helpful orientation toward others; follow promises with actions; maintain confidences and disclose information ethically and appropriately; and conduct work in open, transparent ways.

People are naturally suspicious of those in leadership roles. The greater the distance between individuals and leaders, the more room for interpretation there is and the more likely the leaders may be mistrusted. *Developing trust* is vital for highly effective leadership; in many ways, it is the glue that holds work groups and organizations together. Conversely, mistrust can create a tremendous sinkhole of time and energy on activities irrelevant to the organization's mission.

WHEN HIGHLY EFFECTIVE LEADERS EARN LOYALTY AND TRUST

Given what we have noted about the natural tendency toward suspicion, leaders in some ways start with a "burden of proof." However, leaders can easily rack up trustworthiness points by simply improving their accessibility to staff. The more that leaders are seen as real, authentic people who are accessible and concerned for the problems of their staff and colleagues, the more difficult it will be to view them with suspicion. The following are ways in which exceptional leaders earn their staff's trust.

Being Accessible

Trust development is facilitated when leaders are open, frank, and share information freely. They develop confidences with others and share their feelings—even their fears and concerns. The leaders that people will trust the least are the ones who are cold and distant. Stepping out of the executive suite frequently will lead to enhanced trust.

Fostering Openness

As one well-known CEO once said, "Trust develops over the long haul—there are no quick fixes." Trust begins as leaders and followers gain a sense that each other's actions are predictable. Trust then builds over time in cycles involving increasing familiarity and comfort with interpersonal risk taking. The evolution takes place from both sides of the relationship; leaders take some personal risks when they reveal themselves, and followers take risks when they rely on their leaders.

Exceptional leaders care about their staff and will try to minimize the risk for their followers. They will actively cultivate an environment of considerable psychological safety, in which people feel they can speak openly and honestly without fear of their comments "coming back to haunt" them. Leaders accomplish this not only by demonstrating themselves to be capable of openly receiving feedback but also by thanking their staff for taking the risk to put issues on the table.

Being Authentic

Authenticity is a critical component of trust. Stephen Mickus (2005), president and CEO of Mercy Health Partners in Toledo, Ohio, talks frequently about "engaging both the hearts and minds" of his employees and physicians. He realizes that his ability to engage their hearts and minds requires that they first be *connected* to his own heart and mind. This is the ultimate "walking the talk." Leaders who do this best are like Mickus in that they accept their own personal ability to grow and then live their values by connecting authentically to what they do in their work.

The relationship between care and ability is another aspect of being authentic. Highly effective leaders care about their followers, and the followers know that their leaders have the ability and capability to do what is needed. Trust involves leaders who fulfill their promises; there is what one might call a high "do/say ratio." Staff, physicians, and other stakeholders want to know their leaders are not only willing to do what they say they will but also are *capable* of doing it.

When exceptional leaders learn that they will be unable to keep a promise, they address it as proactively as possible and give people the heads-up right away. Whenever possible, reparations are made, even if the reparations are of a token nature. You can think of this as a symbolic gesture to convey that you take your promises very seriously. Highly effective leaders know the worst response is to say nothing and hope the transgression goes unnoticed. It is most often noticed, and trust takes an extra hit in the process.

Modeling Behavior

Breakthrough leaders demonstrate role modeling throughout all aspects of their workplace interactions. If there are sacrifices to be made, they will step up first. If there are rewards to be doled out, they will allow others to step forward first.

Willingness to chip in is another area that sends a strong, implicit message about the leader's character. By being willing to help out in times of stress or crisis and in handling tasks they normally would not do, leaders communicate their fundamental positive regard for the contributions their coworkers make to the workplace. The implicit message is, "I wouldn't ask you to do anything I wouldn't be willing to do myself."

Indeed, exceptional leaders are just as likely to chip in with the tasks their coworkers enjoy the least as they are to chip in where their contributions will be greatest.

Turning Trust into Loyalty

Trust is best considered a necessary but not sufficient condition for loyalty. Trust becomes loyalty when followers experience the leader as supporting their own interests over a period of time. Exceptional leaders are capable of taking these individual interests and finding ways to bring them into alignment with the organization's goals. As in military parlance, the followers bind themselves to the course of action that is being taken.

WHEN EARNING LOYALTY AND TRUST IS NOT ALL IT COULD BE

As we previously noted, most people are naturally wary of individuals in positions of authority. As such, there is no baseline of loyalty and trust that is automatically granted with a particular leadership role; quite the opposite is true. A person's baseline loyalty is to the role or the job rather than to the leader. Development of trust and loyalty will be impaired if a leader demonstrates any of the following.

Being Unavailable

Some leaders are most comfortable staying in their offices. They may describe themselves as having an open-door policy but may send subtle signals that you had better have a good reason for interrupting them. Leaders who are described as difficult to approach will usually receive less trust from their staff.

Other leaders may engage their staff more regularly but still fail to convey a genuine concern about challenges they are facing. The difference between *having* and *showing* concern is important here: Most leaders have concern, but not all of them are adept at showing it. Some leaders find listening to their staff's complaints so discomforting that they feel compelled either to jump to an immediate fix or to push for a change of subject. While a change of subject has a more obvious effect, the fix approach also fails to convey a true sense of engagement; the message that staff may interpret is, "How can I get this off my to-do list as quickly as possible?"

Still other leaders may show concern to their staff but will fail to "go to bat" for their staff as much as they should. A leader might tell staff, "I'll see what I can do" and then either not follow-up or not circle back to staff to tell them what happened. In both cases, the result is the same: Staff will assume the leader did not care enough to do anything about their concerns.

Lacking Follow-Through

There is perhaps no more frequent barrier to trust building than a lack of follow-through. Lack of follow-through will often appear callous or even malicious, though this is rarely the intent. More often, the cause is an overwillingness to make promises without thinking through what it will take to make good on them. (As one exceptional leader once told us, "The easiest thing for a leader to do is to say yes. The hardest thing to do is to say no.") Other leaders simply have not mastered their organizational skills to the point where they can keep track of what they told people they would do for them.

Of course, we all face situations where we have agreed to do something only to find out later we will not be able to honor that promise. In general, people are forgiving of such transgressions, assuming they do not become regular patterns. However, people are much less forgiving of leaders who do not accept personal responsibility for them.

Assigning Credit or Blame to the Wrong Person

Leaders chip away at trust and loyalty whenever they assign credit or blame to the wrong individuals. Leaders often do this with no willful intention whatsoever. Leaders may simply be in the habit of describing the work of their group by saying, "I" and may forget to acknowledge the team's contributions when they are in the room. Conversely, in the heat of the moment of learning about a failure on the part of team members, some leaders may be quick to harshly

When Earning Loyalty and Trust Is Not All It Could Be

Leaders who do not build trust and loyalty to their full potential may have fallen short as a result of any of the following behaviors:

- Being unavailable
  - Leaders are not available to staff when they are needed and appear unconcerned about staff's challenges.
  - Leaders are unwilling to "go to bat" for staff.

- Lacking follow-through
  - Leaders lose track of what was promised others or makes promises that cannot be delivered.
  - Leaders do not acknowledge these as failures on their part; others are blamed or the failures are not acknowledged at all.

- Assigning credit or blame to the wrong person
  - The contributions of team members are not acknowledged.
  - Personal responsibility for decisions and actions are avoided.

- Failing to lead by example
  - Others are held to standards that the leader does not demonstrate.
  - Leaders are unwilling to go first into "uncharted waters" or to chip in when help is needed.

note individual accountabilities rather than to take the time to fully understand why the failures occurred, or they may fail to understand and acknowledge their own role in the problems.

In the moment, any one of these oversights may seem relatively benign. Over time, however, people get the message that there is a less certain payoff (and, in the case of blame, a greater risk) to the efforts they put forth on that leader's behalf. Typically, they will adjust their efforts accordingly.

Failing to Lead by Example

We define leading by example according to two fundamental behaviors: (1) modeling the approach to work and the workplace that you request of others and (2) being willing to lend one's efforts to the work responsibilities of others.

Over the years, people have begun to interpret the phrase "leading by example" as though it were a description of a particular leadership style. In our view, leading by example is not a style but a practice. Leading by example means that the behavior of leaders corresponds with their statements. For example, autocratic leaders can lead by example; they may be autocratic, but their behavior reliably reflects this style. In similar fashion, participative leaders can lead by example by being participative on a consistent basis. They key is predictability; others must be able to rely on you. Leading by example is essential to highly effective leadership, regardless of the other aspects of the person's style. Indeed, in our review of leadership models, we were unable to identify any that appeared incompatible with leading by example.

Role modeling is fundamental not only to leadership but also to every facet of human relationships. We all are constantly attentive to the social cues of the people we interact with, and we are continuously modifying our behavior accordingly. If a person says one thing and does another, we are more likely to attend to what they did rather than what they said. (We will also be less likely to trust them in the future.) Leaders who do not remember this basic lesson in human nature will be repeatedly undercutting their effectiveness in building relationships of trust.

MISUSE AND OVERUSE: HOW EARNING LOYALTY AND TRUST CAN WORK AGAINST YOU

We have seen a number of instances where leaders have overemphasized loyalty and trust to the eventual detriment of better performance. When this happens, one of the following patterns is usually present.

Communicating Too Directly

On the one hand, open and candid communication is essential to maximizing performance. Without such dialog, performance problems cannot be surfaced and addressed. On the other hand, we all have a self-concept that we guard jealously; we can only handle so much truth about ourselves at once. Leaders who fail to understand this are at risk for overcommunicating about performance deficits, which results in an environment that can feel harsh, punitive, and is simply not enjoyable to work in.

Candor needs to be tempered with considerations about how a feedback message will be received by a given individual or group. A simple but often overlooked tip is to deliver criticism in one-on-one dialog rather than in a group context. Another suggestion is to address interpersonal conflict by first acknowledging the value that the working relationship holds for you.

Discouraging Dissenting Opinions

In some cases, open communication may be viewed as a challenge to loyalty. For example, when substantial organizational change efforts are implemented, such a premium can be put on being on board that dissenting opinions are actively discouraged. In these cases, employees may learn to keep their concerns to themselves for fear of being viewed as disloyal.

In other cases, leaders may be so successful in their compelling communications that employees become overly faithful. Employees may view the leader's actions in purely emotional rather than rational terms, so much so that groupthink begins to set in and they begin to distrust their own independent judgment. Speaking up starts to feel like a failure on their part, and they begin to follow the leader's directives blindly.

Overemphasizing Loyalty

Some leaders may create a cult of personality around their roles such
that loyalty to those leaders is viewed as superordinate to the
mission that the leaders are employed to support. Leaders may place
special emphasis on loyalty, holding it in higher regard than other
elements of job performance more central to the organization's
mission. Sometimes this is done by creating an "us versus them"

mentality within a given group. Not surprisingly, such an approach will often do more to grow the leader's power base than it will to improve the organization; in the long run, the approach is very difficult to sustain at all.

A less insidious but still problematic shortcoming involves leaders who attempt to foster loyalty to their teams by devaluing other groups within the organization. For example, support departments sometimes fall into a pattern of externalizing service problems by blaming the customer. Leaders who fail to challenge (or who may even encourage) the view that other departments are inferior in any way (e.g., less talented, less professional) also indirectly discourage the development of useful cross-departmental working relationships as well as the resolution of challenges the departments may face in working with each other.

WHAT TO DO TO BETTER EARN LOYALTY AND TRUST

Finding Role Models

Although there are many ways one could measure loyalty, one of the most straightforward is employee retention. Within your organization, who has the best record of retaining staff? Have any new leaders to your organization brought a number of people with them? A human resources executive will likely know the answers to these questions and thus may have the names of some good potential role models.

Also consider any specific leaders whom you have trusted greatly. These may be very good people to reconnect with or good experiences to reflect on. What was it exactly about their behavior that inspired that level of trust? What specifically might you do that will help others trust you to that same extent?

Additional Opportunities for Personal Development

It can be very difficult to get an accurate read on the loyalty and trust people have in you. In most cases, the only way to get at this may be to ask people, directly or indirectly, for this feedback. The direct approach involves finding an opportunity to talk with staff one-on-one to ask them about their experiences. Here are some model questions you might use as a starting point, depending on the specific nature of your relationship with the person you are meeting with.

- It's important to me that I follow-through on what I say I will do. I try hard to do this, but I'm probably not perfect. Can you recall any times when I may have missed the mark in the last year?
- I want you to feel that you can talk openly and candidly with me and that I will be respectful of what you tell me. How well would you say I have done in achieving that goal? Are there any situations you can remember in which you would have preferred that I handled things differently?
- I want to make sure that I am being an effective role model in my approach to our work. Of course, it's difficult for me to know how effectively I am coming across to others in that regard. Can you give me some feedback on how I have been as a role model—in particular, any areas in which I might improve?

One of the classic books on trust is Kouzes and Posner's (1993) *Credibility: How Leaders Gain and Lose It, Why People Demand It*. Chapter 2 of their book ("Credibility Makes a Difference") provides a compelling view of leadership from the follower's perspective. In Chapter 7 ("Serving a Purpose"), there is a useful section on losing and regaining credibility. Finally, Dye's (2000) book *Leadership in Healthcare: Values at the Top*, provides additional guidance on developing trust (Chapter 13, pages 111–120).

REFERENCES

Dye, C. 2000. *Leadership in Healthcare: Values at the Top.* Chicago, IL: Health Administration Press.

Kouzes, J. M., and B. Z. Posner. 1993. *Credibility: How Leaders Gain and Lose It, Why People Demand It.* San Francisco: Jossey-Bass.

Mickus, S. L. 2005. Personal communication with authors.

CORNERSTONE 3

Real Way
With People

CHAPTER SIX

Listening Like You Mean It

Jack reviews his notes while he waits for Linda to come out of her office. He has been waiting for almost 20 minutes, but he does not mind too much; he knows she has many other presses on her time, and he is grateful to be having the meeting at all.

Meanwhile, Linda is meeting with her CFO and an outside auditor. The news is not good: The cost overruns on the new building project will likely pull the hospital into the red this quarter. Linda will need to inform the board about that later this week. In the best case scenario, she will hear a few "I told you so" comments. She would rather not think about the worst case scenario.

Linda comes out of the meeting and sees Jack waiting. It has been a long day, but she does not want to put him off again. Jack comes in and excitedly begins outlining an ambitious marketing campaign. A less-seasoned executive, he jumps right to his ideas for splashy TV ads without first building his business case. In her mind, Linda sees only another big sinkhole of cash opening up in front of her. She has already decided she will not support the initiative, but she lets Jack continue out of a mixture of courtesy and inertia. Her silence quickly turns to seething as Jack continues his image-driven presentation; Jack, thinking Linda is growing impatient, picks up his pace. He finishes his presentation with, "I'm getting the sense that the timing isn't right for this. Yes?"

"Yes," says Linda, relieved that Jack arrived at the conclusion himself.

Although this vignette describes a specific exchange between two leaders, the nature of the exchange is common in healthcare: different perspectives coming together awkwardly in a poorly planned, poorly executed meeting. We can see the frustrations and disappointments on both sides, and we can probably relate to the experiences of one or both individuals.

A key facet of this vignette is the lost opportunities for learning, enhancing mutual understanding, and improving performance. The opportunities are lost for lack of better listening skills.

WHAT IS LISTENING LIKE YOU MEAN IT, AND WHY IS IT IMPORTANT?

> **Listening like you mean it** means you maintain a calm, easy-to-approach demeanor; are patient, open minded, and willing to hear people out; understand others and pick up the meaning of their messages; are warm, gracious, and inviting; build strong rapport; see through the words that others express to the real meaning (i.e., cut to the heart of the issue); and maintain formal and informal channels of communication.

Listening like you mean it distinguishes true active listening from all other forms. Many people like to think of themselves as good listeners, but we all know there is a difference between waiting for your turn to talk and really hearing what a person is trying to say to you. Listening, and demonstrating that you are listening, are skills that can be cultivated. As a leader, it is worth your while to do so; it will improve the trust people put in you, and it will increase your value to your organization because you will be better able to effectively implement strategy.

Active listening improves a leader's effectiveness in several key ways. Perhaps foremost, the investment in listening can help you to better understand the goals, priorities, and perspectives of the people you work with. This equips you to have more helpful and more meaningful dialogs about the work you do together, which in turn can foster deeper levels of interpersonal trust.

Listening also pays dividends in facilitating your role as a change agent. With a better mental map of your peers, direct reports, and superiors, you will have an easier time understanding how individuals relate to their work as well as how organizational changes can help and harm them. When you propose changes, you will have an easier time anticipating fears and concerns and addressing them proactively. This capacity for problem solving affords these leaders an easier time creating and sustaining high-energy organizations.

WHEN HIGHLY EFFECTIVE LEADERS LISTEN LIKE THEY MEAN IT

Highly effective listeners grasp a great deal from a speaker's message. However, they also grasp a lot from the messenger. Exceptional leaders understand the motivations behind the message and value the speaker's unique perspective.

Understanding the Message

Beyond the surface content, highly effective listeners will also understand the why behind the message—what it is about the speaker that has led to the statement, presentation, or request. They will hear the emotion or passion, and they will perceive the level of concurrence or disagreement in the ongoing dialog.

In honing your listening skills, it is helpful to keep in mind that every message is crafted by a person who is trying to get a set of needs met—perhaps her own, the department's, or the patient's. These speakers are expressing needs and revealing something about themselves in the hope that the listener will understand them.

Valuing the Messenger

What if the message is one you disagree with? Effective listeners will still demonstrate they value and respect the thoughts, opinions, and ideas of speakers. In expressing disagreement, they will present the possibility that the speaker's perspective is valid and make the speaker feel heard. Rather than say the speaker is wrong, effective listeners will view the disagreement as a difference in opinion or perspective: something to be explored in such a way that both parties gain a better understanding of each other.

WHEN LISTENING LIKE YOU MEAN IT IS NOT ALL IT COULD BE

Leaders often vary widely in their listening effectiveness depending on the circumstances at hand. The following are some of the ways listening can fall short of being effective, and why.

Listening Inattentively

You can think of inattentiveness in listening as how generally easy or difficult it is to communicate with someone. This is often a more global issue about how leaders set up their workdays and their orientations toward the people they work with. Some leaders inherently enjoy interacting with people throughout the day; others prefer working in solitude. Leaders with the latter tendency (sometimes referred to as introverts) are particularly vulnerable to problems with inattentive listening. They may send indirect messages that they would rather not be bothered, or they may appear impatient when people do seek them out.

Another type of inattentiveness can arise from failing to set up dependable communication channels. Leaders who do not set up regular meetings with their staff (or who routinely cancel them) or who do not reliably respond to voicemails or e-mails can create the same implicit (albeit unintended) message to others: Your communications are not that important to me.

Hearing Selectively

Hearing selectively refers to the tendency to tune out information the listener disagrees with. We all have this tendency to some degree. In fact, some measure of this tendency is probably functional; leaders do not have the luxury to stop in their tracks every time someone disagrees with them to work through the disagreement on the spot. However, this tendency also works against us in two important ways: (1) it can prevent us from being able to take in useful new information and (2) it can prevent us from taking an appropriate amount of time to acknowledge divergent opinions as having some legitimacy. Taking the time to understand *why* a staff member does not agree with you can be an important part of building and maintaining the working relationship. People are usually less upset by being disagreed with than by being dismissed.

When Listening Like You Mean It
Is Not All It Could Be

In leadership roles, listening can fall short for any of the
following reasons:

■ Listening inattentively

- Direct reports are given the impression that their
  communications are bothersome intrusions.

- Few or no routine settings in which listening can take
  place are provided.

■ Hearing selectively

- Divergent opinions are ignored.

- Time is spent formulating counterarguments rather
  than listening.

■ Being impatient

- The listener jumps to erroneous conclusions and cuts
  people off prematurely.

- The listener changes the subject rather than
  concludes it.

■ Being emotionally volatile

- The listener reacts with visible anger, disgust, or
  disappointment.

■ Providing time rather than attention

- The listener is effective at taking turns but substitutes
  silence for genuine listening.

- The focus is on formulating rebuttals rather than on
  taking in what is being said.

Being Impatient

Impatience is a pervasive barrier to effective listening. Almost all leaders in healthcare work under extraordinary time pressures, and listening can sometimes feel unproductive. The ever-present temptation is to find ways to "listen more efficiently." Efficiency can be virtuous, but it is often pursued in the wrong ways.

In situations of acute time pressure, effective leaders will tell speakers how much time they have available so the speaker can manage that time wisely. The less effective approach is to try to reach a speaker's conclusion before the speaker is finished talking. This might involve finishing the speaker's sentences or, even worse, assuming you have the "gist" of it and simply cutting the comments off and taking your own turn. In some uncomfortable dialogs or ones in which the leader cannot productively respond in the moment the leader may even change the subject without warning.

Being Emotionally Volatile

Emotional volatility goes by a number of names: "short fuse" and "hair trigger" come to mind. It represents a very basic failure of listening in that the leader's emotions are overtaking their ability to objectively hear what the speaker is saying.

The consequences of being volatile can be quite drastic. At a minimum, it decreases people's trust to the point that they may actively hide bad news from the leader to avoid being scolded. At worst, it will cause people to withdraw from the working relationship altogether.

Providing Time Rather than Attention

Some leaders master the art of "listening without listening." They do all the right things to ensure their peers and direct reports have adequate access to them, and they do not rush people or cut them off. But the listening is ultimately a façade; silence is provided for politeness' sake, with all mental energy wandering elsewhere or formulating rebuttals rather than considering what the speaker has to say.

MISUSE AND OVERUSE: HOW LISTENING LIKE YOU MEAN IT CAN WORK AGAINST YOU

It is difficult to conceive of leaders getting themselves into trouble for listening too much. Indeed, former U.S. president Calvin Coolidge was famously quoted as saying, "No man ever listened himself out of a job." In our experience, if leaders are viewed as overdoing it on listening, it is usually because they are engaging in one of the following.

Taking Too Passive an Approach to Listening

Some leaders do not actively manage the listening process enough. An example that most of us can relate to is a meeting in which the conveners provide too little structure, allowing individuals to monopolize the dialog and/or direction of the process. Leaders who are overly focused on avoiding disagreements may also fall into this passive pattern. Such leaders may allow others to "air their views" but will offer no public challenge to them, even if they hold conflicting views. In the end, these leaders will do what they originally intended, leaving those around them with puzzling mixed messages.

Using Listening to Avoid Action

When leaders are faced with difficult decisions, listening can sometimes become a stall tactic. Collecting stakeholder opinions is an important step in many difficult decisions, but it is also a step that can be overdone. If you have ever been involved in a never-ending survey process (i.e., a survey that leads only to the conclusion that additional surveys are needed), then you are familiar with this dynamic.

> **Misuse and Overuse: How Listening Like You Mean It Can Work Against You**
>
> Listening is rarely viewed as an overused skill. However, perceived overuse is usually a symptom of one of the following problems:
>
> ■ Taking too passive an approach to listening
>   - People are allowed to "take the podium" without regard to time or efficiency, particularly in meetings.
>   - Points of disagreement are not expressed or explored.
>
> ■ Using listening to avoid action
>   - The leader listens too acutely when a decision must be made (and may not listen enough at other times).
>   - The need for additional input, opinions, and discussion is overly encouraged.

WHAT TO DO TO IMPROVE LISTENING LIKE YOU MEAN IT

Finding Role Models

Where do you find good listening mentors—people who can help you hone your listening skills? One approach is to look for people who are professionally trained in listening, such as counselors and therapists. However, while these professionals may be terrific listeners, they may not be as effective at balancing listening against other time constraints. People who are likely to be good at balancing attention against time include executives in human resources management, marketing and communications, and philanthropy and development. These roles often involve the need to carefully attend to agendas that may or may not be compelling or personally relevant, and that they may personally disagree with, and often under considerable associated time constraints.

Additional Opportunities for Personal Development

We recommend to all readers, no matter how seasoned, that they seriously consider working on their listening skills. Our experiences and those of others who provided input for this chapter suggest most of us have more room for improvement in this area than we may believe and will see more payoff from improving these skills than we may realize.

As with many of the skills discussed in this book, the best approach to improving your listening skills involves a small amount of education and large amounts of practice with feedback.

Seek Feedback

Feedback is essential for rapidly developing listening skills. None of us is consistently a highly effective or ineffective listener. Depending on factors such as the topic, audience, and time of day, we may do better or worse. Also, because ineffective listening is never our goal, it is hard for us to initially pinpoint when we are listening more or less effectively.

Trusted colleagues can be very helpful in this regard. If someone says to you that he feels like you do not listen to him, ask him to help you identify specific examples. Start by looking backward, but then ask also for his help in moving forward.

If a colleague agrees to give you this feedback, pledge to yourself to work extra hard to capitalize on it. If he has genuinely caught you at a listening low point, thank him for his help. If there are other circumstances that you feel prevent you from taking the time to listen, take the time to at least explain these to him: "I see how you didn't have the chance to finish describing your concerns. Unfortunately, your description was putting the meeting agenda behind, and I felt we needed to move on."

Develop a Clear, Active Listening Posture

Displaying active listening involves more than silence—body language also plays a substantial role. If you have ever seen someone roll their eyes after hearing something, you have a sense of body language associated with poor listening; others include checking the time, sighing loudly, or looking away. Body language associated with effective listening includes facing the person who is talking, sitting up straight, maintaining good eye contact, nodding in acknowledgment, or reacting to key points the speaker is making, and taking notes.

Summarize

Summarizing is a particularly useful technique in situations where your own opinions disagree strongly with someone else's. In these situations, challenge yourself to summarize the speaker's comments back to him: "If I understand you correctly, you think you are more qualified for this project than I am because you have prior experience with their department's VP, and I do not. Is that correct?" Forcing yourself to take this step serves several goals. First, and most importantly, it forces you to listen to what the other person is saying at a deep enough level that you are able to represent it back. Second, it helps you decentralize from your own perspective long enough to gain a glimpse of the speaker's perspective. Third, if you still disagree with the speaker, he should no longer believe it is because of a lack of your understanding of his perspective.

Summarizing can also be helpful in less-heated dialogs. You can think of them as checkpoints that provide you with the opportunity to be sure you and others are still proceeding with a common understanding.

Ask Probing Questions

Probing questions are follow-up questions designed to elicit a deeper understanding of a subject—thus the term probe. One style of probing, requesting specifics, focuses on clarifying the message: "You said employees are upset about this change. How many employees are we talking about? How upset are they? Do they want to resign?

Do they feel betrayed or merely inconvenienced? How would you compare their reactions to the premium increase (or other example) —stronger, weaker, or about the same?" A time-based probe can help clarify whether an issue seems to be a flare-up versus an ongoing trend that may be building steam: "How long has this been going on? How consistent has the trend been?"

Monitor Your Emotions

Strong emotional reactions can quickly derail good listening practices. This can play out in several common ways.

- *Shock*. You might react with shock when you find news or ideas difficult to believe. In these situations, it is important to guard against the tendency to dismiss the information or to react too strongly to it. A good way to handle this reaction is to put it on the table in a nonthreatening way: "This comes as a surprise to me. I may need a few minutes to take this in."
- *Anger or disgust*. Reactions of anger and disgust can happen when you believe someone is thinking or acting incompetently or in a way that is not in the best interests of your department or organization. In these situations, there is often a need to convey an important learning point or to foster a better understanding between yourself and the other person; however, this need may be competing with an instinctive feeling of threat and a commensurate reflex to strike back. A more moderate, and typically more effective approach, is to use questions instead of attacks: "Can you help me understand how this would positively affect our department?" or "How would this resolve the problem?"
- *Elation*. We can all come up with examples of when our negative feelings toward someone else interfered with our ability to attend to their communication. The same is true about positive emotions. If you find yourself getting overly excited about an idea, you may find your own internal thought process triggering at such a fast pace that you lose the bead on what is being said.

- *Boredom.* A reaction of boredom most often comes from judging the communication to be irrelevant, unimportant, or not delivered efficiently (e.g., over elaboration on details). Sometimes, particularly if the speaker is anxious, both the communicator and the listener will be well served by some assistance in framing the message: "Let me see if I am understanding the heart of the matter here." Other times, however, the meta-communication you may need to hear is, "I want to feel you value my opinion and will take the time to hear me out." In these cases, the challenge is more internal: Find the anchors to keep yourself appropriately and mentally engaged in the dialog. Balancing your focus between the content of the message and the personal meaning behind the content can be a useful approach.

Schedule Time with Smaller Groups

Large group meetings, while effective for many purposes, do limit participants' comfort in disclosing points of disagreement. You can facilitate the flow of feedback by finding occasions to meet with smaller groups of staff. Smaller group meetings also allow you more opportunities to build individual relationships of trust.

Find Opportunities for One-on-One Conversation

Just as small group meetings can enhance feedback over large groups, so too can one-on-one communication over small groups. Think for a moment about the people you count on most in your organization. Do you have opportunities to meet with each of them individually on a periodic basis? If you do not, you should consider finding these opportunities from time to time. Meeting with someone individually gives you a unique opportunity to reflect not just on the work you do with this person but also on the quality of your working relationship.

Visit the Troops

Highly effective listening involves going beyond a "my door is open" policy to a "let me knock on your door" policy. While staff usually appreciate responsiveness of their leaders to concerns they express, there are few actions that demonstrate concern more concretely than planned and purposeful visits to worksites.

Mind Your Limits

Despite your best efforts, there may be times when you will not be as effective a listener as you would like to be. Fatigue can be a barrier to effective listening—for example, at the end of a hard day, week, or after difficult conversations or disappointments. Another key barrier is role conflict—someone coming to talk with you about a concern at a time when your mind is firmly pointed elsewhere, or when you need to be preparing for your next meeting.

How you handle those situations depends partly on your ability to overcome your fatigue or distraction, as well as how fatigued you are. On the one hand, concentration, like other skills, improves with practice—if you push yourself to listen through your fatigue, you will continue to get better at it. For this reason, taking the time to listen can sometimes be better than putting a conversation off.

However, there may be times when you are too tired or distracted to have any hope of listening effectively. In these situations, efforts to overcome your fatigue will not pay off, and it is better to delay the conversation diplomatically. You can do so by first acknowledging the importance of what the speaker has to say before requesting a postponement: "I can see this is an important concern to you, and it deserves my full attention. However, right now I won't be able to give you the attention you deserve. I will be too distracted by this meeting coming up later today. I'd like to find a time when I can give you my undivided attention on this matter. What does tomorrow morning look like for you?"

CHAPTER SEVEN

Giving Feedback

It is 11:20 a.m., and the executive leadership team is waiting for Marla to arrive for their weekly meeting. Marla is still relatively new to the leadership group, having been promoted to the chief nursing officer (CNO) role only a few months ago after the unexpected departure of the prior CNO. Several years earlier, the leadership team had established a strict promptness rule for their meetings, resulting in these meetings starting and ending on time. The leadership team cannot get started without her, so the other members use the time however they can—checking back with the office, reading e-mails, or pulling other members out into the hall for conversations. When Marla finally arrives, she looks frustrated. She stomps in, sits down, lets out a loud sigh, and says, "OK, let's go."

Clearly, it is taking all of Marla's energy and patience to learn this new role, and she is doing a reasonably good job with it overall. The rest of the team knows this, and so no one wants to say anything to her about coming in late.

The meeting continues but time runs out before the last agenda item is addressed—an action item from Rick, the general counsel, concerning a risk management strategy he wants the group to support—is cleared. Jeff, the CEO, recognizes there will not be adequate time to discuss the item and suggests tabling it until the following week. Rick, who is now furious, turns to Marla and says, "I want you to remember we did not get to this item because you couldn't be bothered to come to this meeting when you were supposed to. If we get into a malpractice problem this week, I hope you feel personally responsible for the damage you have caused!" (For the record, Marla's response to Rick, who she now views as a pompous "know it all," was even less measured.)

This vignette describes a number of places in which the delivery of feedback was not nearly as effective as it could have been. Marla's failure to come to this meeting on time is inconveniencing her peers and impairing the productivity of the team. However, the team has been reluctant to address the problem with Marla, at least in part because of their sympathy with the challenges she is facing in her new role. In fact, no one had told Marla of the timeliness rule set years earlier. When Marla finally does receive feedback, it is too caustic to be effectively "heard" and leads instead to an unproductive counterattack.

However, this team can hardly be described as dysfunctional. They are productively moving the hospital forward, and over time Marla is successfully learning her role. However, with better approaches to giving and receiving feedback, it is likely Marla would adapt to her role more rapidly, and the team's decision making processes could become even more efficient.

WHAT IS GIVING FEEDBACK, AND WHY IS IT IMPORTANT?

Feedback can be most concisely defined as the delivery of information about performance. For our purposes, we are referring to interpersonal feedback, which is feedback that is transmitted from one individual to another.

> **Giving feedback** means you set clear expectations, bring important issues to the table in a way that helps others "hear" them, show an openness to facing difficult topics and sources of conflict, deal with problems and difficult people directly and frankly, provide timely criticism when needed, and provide feedback messages that are clear and unambiguous.

If you have ever taken a human resources or leadership skills course, you have probably learned some rules of thumb about delivering feedback. Some useful and familiar guidelines are to give feedback as soon as possible after the behavior, to describe objectively what you observed, to suggest a specific course of improvement, and to end on a positive note. All are good tips for feedback, but they are less helpful in thinking through context: the relationship in which the feedback takes place.

Interpersonal feedback messages *always* occur within the context of a relationship. We choose whom we want to give feedback to and when, based on our prior knowledge of the person and how we think he will react. The receiver's reactions, in turn, will be governed by her self-concept and expectations about us. If leaders fail to recognize and draw on these relationship factors in setting up the feedback they provide, the feedback may still work—but it will usually lack the power and utility that it might have had.

WHEN HIGHLY EFFECTIVE LEADERS GIVE FEEDBACK

Leaders with exceptional feedback skills are better at attending to contextual factors. Whenever they are considering providing feedback, they will routinely start with an examination of their own motives by working through the following process.

Defining the Real Issue

Highly effective leaders know that the core issue and the appropriate target for feedback may not be the same as the presenting problem. Too often, busy leaders are not explicit when defining problems. They often dance around the meaning and fail to use precise words. In contrast, highly effective leaders zero-in on the real issues and focus on the true concerns by using more specific and direct language. For example, let us return to our vignette, in which Rick told Marla off for being "discourteous." Had Rick taken more time to think about why he was upset, he may have gained a better understanding of the complex context in which these events were occurring. For instance, perhaps he was resentful of being last on the agenda, which he may have taken to mean that the CEO did not care as much as he should about risk management. Or perhaps Rick had bitten his tongue about Marla's lateness in the past, and he was now reacting to the pattern more so than to the individual event. In failing to recognize either of these possibilities, Rick's feedback is probably far out of proportion to Marla's offense.

Evaluating the Issue

Exceptional leaders ask themselves if the *return* on addressing the issue is likely to be higher than the *cost* of addressing it. One leadership development book featured a section entitled, "Feedback: Give It Often." We disagree with this premise. Highly effective leaders assess the value or return of an issue when discussing it with the individual involved. They often let matters drop because of their lack of importance in the overall scheme of things. One wise CEO once said, "You have to determine if the juice is worth the squeeze." This evaluation is less straightforward than it may initially sound because of how subjective it can be.

In the vignette, Jeff might have chosen to let the lateness issue fester because of his own fears that he will cause Marla to resign the role. If this were indeed a legitimate concern, it may make sense to have allowed passive support win out over constructive feedback. (In reality, the likelihood that Marla would resign over this feedback is probably quite low.) Conversely, leaders can sometimes view some behaviors as more problematic than they really are. Such a leader might address both a misspelling in an e-mail and a careless patient safety violation with the same harsh tone.

Setting the Stage

Once a decision has been made to deliver feedback, highly effective leaders will make sure they give adequate thought to setting the stage for delivery. If the climate of the discussion is "safe," there is a much better chance the receivers will be able to accept the feedback without getting overly defensive and productively use it in improving their performance. If the leader is particularly upset, she may feel unable to deliver the feedback in a measured way and will delay the conversation.

Balancing Feedback

Highly effective leaders make sure the people they work with receive a good balance of positive and constructive feedback. Some go as far as to mentally "pencil in" a small chunk of time during the workday to develop and deliver positive feedback to their staff. People appreciate receiving positive feedback, which is perhaps reason enough to pursue this practice, but positive feedback also serves another purpose: It helps staff have greater resilience to the constructive feedback they receive. If a person feels like they are generally doing okay, they will usually feel less of a sense of personal vulnerability when they receive constructive feedback and will be more able to hear and productively use the feedback they receive.

WHEN GIVING FEEDBACK IS NOT ALL IT COULD BE

Problems with the delivery of feedback can stem from motivation or from the need for better methods. Here are some common reasons why feedback can fall short.

Being Reluctant to Critique

Some leaders view critiques as punitive measures and will avoid them until they feel they have no other option. This bias can be compounded by the reality that many healthcare staff work extraordinarily long hours and under considerable pressure—what kind of monster would needlessly add pain and suffering to the mix?

In reality, critiques are needlessly painful only if they are delivered poorly or too infrequently. The latter is a lesson often associated with the "wait and see" approach (i.e., holding off on giving

When Giving Feedback Is Not All It Could Be

In leadership roles, listening can fall short for any of the following reasons:

- Being reluctant to critique
  - Critiques are viewed as punishments and not delivered until someone "really deserves it."
  - There is a bias toward the "wait and see approach" for performance problems.

- Hesitating to praise
  - There is a failure to provide positive feedback as a routine part of work.
  - Leaders are reluctant to deliver praise except in very unusual circumstances.

- Structuring feedback poorly
  - Critiques are too focused on the individual rather than on the problem behavior or performance.
  - Feedback is delivered with too much or too little force or is too vague.

- Giving judgmental feedback
  - Critiques are focused on the "why" of the behavior rather than the "what."
  - The feedback recipient's defensiveness distracts him from "hearing" the feedback.

feedback in the hope that the performance problem will self-correct). When the problem persists, a leader may not only be on the hook for confronting the problem but also for explaining why there is a sudden interest in a problem that has persisted for so long.

Hesitating to Praise

At least as frequent a problem, if not more frequent, is a hesitancy to praise. Leadership roles tend to focus on fixing things, and it is easy to forget to notice what is going well. Most leaders will acknowledge extraordinary performance, but the praise is typically expected in such situations and has less of an emotional impact on the recipient than receiving praise for routine, successful performance.

Structuring Feedback Poorly

Feedback can also fall short if it is not well delivered. If the focus is too narrow, it may not be taken seriously by the recipient; if too wide, it can come across as an attack. If it is too vague, the recipient will leave feeling puzzled, or worse helpless, as to how to improve.

Another important consideration is the amount of emotional force behind the message. As the saying goes, "Leaders cast long shadows"; what feels like a slap on the wrist in delivery can come across like a bullet in receipt. Conversely, leaders who find themselves in great pain when delivering critiques may overly sugarcoat the message and then feel frustrated when the recipient does not seem concerned about the problem performance.

Giving Judgmental Feedback

Sometimes it is difficult to focus a feedback message just on the behavior, particularly when the behavior is either part of an ongoing pattern or seems so commonsense that it is hard to believe the person would not know better. However, going any deeper than the observed behavior can quickly render a feedback message less effective; it creates a level of defensiveness that becomes a potent distracter from the feedback itself. Exceptional leaders are certain to describe the situation factually, refrain from expressing opinions or value judgments, and focus on the actual behavior and consequences (i.e., keep focused on the "what" of the situation); on the other hand, less effective leaders tend to create a debate about the "why."

MISUSE AND OVERUSE: HOW GIVING FEEDBACK CAN WORK AGAINST YOU

For leaders who are described as giving too much feedback, often one or more of the following patterns is present.

Giving Feedback Too Quickly

Some leaders have too much of a "hair trigger" when it comes to delivering feedback. Leaders who do not stop to ask themselves, "Is this an issue worth addressing?" fall into this category. In a similar vein, leaders can be too quick to jump to action after hearing about problems from a third party. If leaders do not first inquire about the "offender's" side of the story, they set themselves up for a lot of defensiveness from the feedback receiver.

Delivering Feedback Too Frequently

It is possible to give feedback too often. This can happen when leaders have unrealistic expectations about performance improvement. Some skills and behaviors, particularly the more complex and ingrained ones, take more effort to change than we realize. The best antidote is to set mutually agreed-on goals and timelines for performance improvement and to limit constructive feedback on the focal issue during the interim periods. For some leaders, the subjective loss of control associated with "backing off" for a while is too much to bear. If this is the case, the leader's need for excessive control may be the real issue that should be addressed.

Misuse and Overuse: How Giving Feedback Can Work Against You

Leaders are sometimes described as giving too much feedback. Typically, that will look like one or more of the following:

■ Giving feedback too quickly

  • Attention is drawn toward unimportant performance problems.

  • Feedback is based on hearsay alone.

■ Delivering feedback too frequently

  • The leader has unrealistic expectations about the velocity of performance improvement.

  • Feedback is used as an excuse for micromanagement.

■ Giving imbalanced feedback

  • There is an overemphasis on constructive feedback and a lack of positive feedback.

  • Critiques are delivered with too strong a tone or emphasis.

Giving Imbalanced Feedback

Sometimes when leaders are described as providing "too much feedback," the real concern is an imbalance between positive and negative feedback. Positive feedback often helps staff to be more resilient to critiques; conversely, if they are not receiving positive feedback, the critiques sting more. Of course, the imbalance can also happen on the positive side; some leaders indeed overuse the "strokes" to the point where they come across as perfunctory or gratuitous. If this is the case, it may suggest some general limitations in a leader's ability to "read" her direct reports.

HOW TO BE BETTER AT GIVING FEEDBACK

Finding Role Models

Because so much of the most transformative feedback happens one on one, identifying mentors in this area can be difficult. The best approach may be peer nomination: Ask people who they would identify as particularly good at providing feedback. Another approach is to ask a senior human resources executive for his recommendations; he should have both the mental framework for such an assessment as well as the broad knowledge of leaders in your institution to allow him to make informed suggestions.

Additional Opportunities for Personal Development

The best way to learn more skillful feedback approaches is to simply practice and to get feedback yourself. Often the best place to start is with someone you already feel you have a very solid working relationship with. Enlist this person's help in crafting effective feedback dialogs. You might also ask them to role play with you any particularly challenging feedback sessions you need to have with others.

If you think you need to provide more positive feedback in addition to your critiques, try setting aside five minutes per day for this specific task. You might add this as a note in your PDA or on your calendar. At first, the exercise may feel forced, but over time you should find it easier to identify positive things your staff have done and find opportunities to express your appreciation.

For managing the delivery of constructive feedback in the context of your relationship with others, we recommend the book *Crucial Conversations* by Kerry Patterson and colleagues (2002). Their organization has been analyzing effective feedback and communication for many years; their recommendations are based on intensive fieldwork and are usually on target.

REFERENCE

Patterson, K., J. Grenny, R. McMillan, and A. Switzler. 2002. *Crucial Conversations: Tools for Talking When Stakes Are High*. New York: McGraw-Hill.

CHAPTER EIGHT

Mentoring Others

Denise was new to the role of vice president of clinical services, but she knew full well the challenges she would be facing in the coming years. Most of the department heads had long tenures in their roles, and many had become complacent during the long string of sound financial times. Some were very good with their people skills but not as strong with their financial ones. Others had great budgeting and revenue management skills but failed to invest appropriately in leadership development programs, often to the detriment of their staff. There also were a host of individual challenges: one department head always hired from the outside and never promoted staff; another was not able to retain people, and still another seemed to spend more time in grievance hearings than he did in meetings with his staff.

The previous vice president of clinical services had been more of a public figure—a visible presence in the community but scarcely available to his direct reports. He took a laissez-faire approach to his staff: "Perform well, and I'll leave you alone; perform poorly, and you're out of here." Denise knew she would need to take a different approach.

In this vignette, Denise has concluded that a number of her new direct reports are underperforming due at least in part to a variety of skills deficits. Denise has the advantage of being a newcomer; there are no roles to renegotiate or habits on her part to unlearn. She also faces a number of challenges: She may not have the time to meet regularly with everyone who could benefit from additional mentoring, and she may herself not have some of the skills her direct reports need to learn. Beyond these basic concerns are a host of more subtle considerations: how strongly should she push people; who should she give "slack" to; how long should she give it to them; and how should she ensure mentoring is deepening, rather than weakening, her working relationships. Exceptional leaders can often be distinguished from good leaders according to how well they navigate these types of challenges.

WHAT IS MENTORING OTHERS, AND WHY IS IT IMPORTANT?

In this context, we define *mentoring others* as all of the actions leaders take to support the long-term growth of their direct reports. Of particular concern are the career goals these individuals have. Do staff members feel they are moving ahead in their jobs and careers? Are they able to expand their responsibilities, either in their present positions or in expanded positions? Do they feel free to openly explore opportunities in other areas of the organization or even outside the organization?

We focus particular attention on the relationship and the goals rather than the means because the activities will differ depending both on the direct report's needs and the leader's capabilities to personally address those needs.

> **Mentoring others** means you invest the time to understand the career aspirations of your direct reports, work with direct reports to create engaging mentoring plans, support staff in developing their skills, support career development in a nonpossessive way (e.g., will support staff moving up and out as necessary for their advancement), find stretch assignments and other delegation opportunities that support skill development, and role model professional development by advancing your own skills.

Returning to the vignette, Denise's framing of her direct reports' performance problems leads to the logical conclusion that a focus on mentoring is necessary. However, in our experience, providing mentoring is a staple for all exceptional leaders, not just for those in situations that so obviously need this attention. This is the case regardless of the overall performance level of the department or organization; in fact, mentoring is more likely to happen in teams that are already high performing—it may be how they got that way in the first place.

WHEN HIGHLY EFFECTIVE LEADERS MENTOR OTHERS

In our experience, the following qualities are hallmarks of mentorship in highly effective people.

Taking a Comprehensive Approach

The most effective mentors focus attention on *all* of their direct reports. Let us return again to the vignette that started this chapter. Although Denise recognizes the need to mentor this group of leaders, she appears to be in some danger of falling into a common trap: focusing on the "problem children." The departments that are in the red are likely to be the ones she herself will be under scrutiny for, so a bias toward attending to these groups is understandable. But what about the departments that are performing well? In addition to fixing problems, a highly effective mentor will also seek ways to make good departments great and to turn great departments into world-class operations.

Building on Relationships

To be a highly effective mentor, your direct reports must come to believe their individual interests will be well served by listening to you. The first step in this process is developing a clear understanding of your direct reports' interests and goals. Mentoring will be most powerful when it focuses on individuals' needs as well as the needs of the organization.

Highly effective leaders meet routinely with each of their direct reports to explore career goals. Once they gain an understanding of how individuals would like to see their jobs, careers, and areas of accountability over the next several years, they can then discuss areas for improvement, simultaneously looking for ways by which these improvements can also serve the individual's goals.

Emphasizing Clear, Consistent Follow-Through

As our emphasis on the relationship suggests, high-performance mentoring requires a long-term commitment to the process. In addition to starting strong, exceptional leaders robustly build the mentoring process into their workflow. Many of these leaders have regularly scheduled meetings with their direct reports to focus on mentoring; the meetings may not be frequent, but they are held consistently.

Participating in Staff Development

In a high-performance approach to staff development, the leader will actively work with staff on skill development. For example, if an off-site educational program is called for, the leader will have some involvement in helping the staff select an appropriate one. When the program is complete, the leader will find time to discuss what was learned with the staff; forethought will also be given to opportunities in which the new skills could be practiced on the job.

Encouraging Growth

Exceptional leaders recognize that higher performing staff are also more employable elsewhere, but that does not stop them from developing their staff. They understand that the value of being viewed as a powerful mentor exceeds the cost of replacing staff when they outgrow their roles. How can this be? Consider the references coming from previous employees. A job with a strong mentor is described as a valuable learning opportunity—one that helped them prepare for the even better position they now hold. A job with a weak mentor is described as a dead end—one that the former staff members "escaped" to accept their new position (which, even worse, may have been a lateral move.)

WHEN MENTORING OTHERS IS NOT ALL IT COULD BE

There are several common conditions in which mentoring is not as effective as it might be. The ones we have encountered most frequently include the following.

Undervaluing Mentoring

If leaders do not view mentoring as an essential part of their roles, chances are it will fall by the wayside. For some leaders, the driving force is left too much in the hands of their staff; they mentor the direct reports who make a point of demanding it, and they are far less attentive to everyone else. The typical result is that the high performers continue to develop their skills, the low performers are ignored until they become serious problems, and the B players never get any better. Some leaders do not even make the initial investment in learning their staff's career goals—or, if they do, they fail to internalize them or at least write them down somewhere accessible.

Another way mentoring can fall short is if leaders view mentorship as events rather than as relationships. We see this in leaders whose automatic reactions to performance improvement needs are to send staff to an off-site conference, workshop, or class. While these approaches can be very helpful in improving knowledge, they usually do little to develop skills and even less to ensure that skills transfer successfully to the staff's workplace.

Undervaluing Staff Development

Some leaders take a more fatalistic "you either have it or you don't" view of skill development. These leaders may not have well-developed abilities to track performance improvement over time, or they may take an overly informal approach to this process. As a result, these leaders tend to think performance levels are more static than they really are.

For some leaders, this tendency shows up as a bias toward replacing people rather than mentoring them. In senior-level positions in particular, many organizations show a bias toward hiring outside talent rather than developing it from within.

When Mentoring Is Not All It Could Be

Mentoring can fall short of optimal for any of the following reasons:

- Undervaluing mentoring
  - Professional and career development is viewed as the responsibility of the individual.
  - Staff's career goals are not tracked.
  - There is a bias toward event-driven development (e.g., sending staff to workshops).
- Undervaluing staff development
  - The leader takes a short-term view of her staff.
  - There is a bias toward "buying" rather than "making" talent.
- Being too possessive
  - The leader is overly concerned about staff outgrowing positions or being poached by another department.
- Lacking mentoring skills
  - The leader lacks a clear sense of how mentoring works, and what his role in mentoring should be.
  - On-the-job opportunities to develop staff's skills are not recognized.

Being Too Possessive

Yet another limitation can arise when leaders are overly possessive of their staff. Some leaders actively avoid mentoring staff out of fear that they will outgrow their positions and leave. Other leaders create barriers to their staff working on some developmental projects out of a fear that other departments will poach them.

Lacking Mentoring Skills

Mentoring can also fall short because of a lack of skills in the mentoring process itself. Some of these skills relate back to our discussion on feedback in Chapter 7. Others relate to the leader's ability to recognize the naturally occurring opportunities for direct reports to develop skills.

Let us consider the latter point in more depth. Think about how you decide who does what in your own department or organization. Chances are, most work goes to the individuals you believe will do the best job, either because of past experiences or relevant skills. Indeed, our industry's approach to human resources is essentially designed to ensure that this is the case. With this in mind, it becomes easier to see how mentoring involves some unnatural approaches to work, at least on occasion. From the mentoring perspective, the question is not always "Who will be most *successful* at this task?" but rather "Who stands to *learn* the most from working on this task?"

MISUSE AND OVERUSE: HOW MENTORING OTHERS CAN WORK AGAINST YOU

If mentoring was taken to the logical extreme, we would no longer have a place of productive work. Instead, we would have a place of education. Of course, an organization can only stay in business if the economic contributions of staff exceed the size of their paychecks, so the learning aspects of a job can only be taken so far. The ideal balance finds the "sweet spot" that maximizes both organizational performance and individual development. But when this balance either leans too far toward mentoring or is not well executed, the following pitfalls might be seen.

Miscommunicating Developmental Decisions

Developing highly effective mentoring relationships requires regular communication, and sometimes not just with the individual receiving the mentoring. Direct reports are often quick to view learning opportunities, even developmental assignments, as being doled out unfairly. Developmental decisions often make good sense, but their rationale is not well communicated to staff. In these situations, sometimes the best remedy is simply to better articulate how these decisions are made, attending in particular to any skill development needs that a staff member may feel are not receiving appropriate attention. However, leaders should also avoid dismissing concerns about fairness too quickly; uneven attention to developmental needs is a reality in many leadership teams.

Overemphasizing Star Performers

When it comes to mentoring, star performers represent a mixed blessing. On the one hand, they tend to yield the highest returns on time their leaders invest in them. On the other, they tend to receive more of the leaders' focus to the detriment of other staff. Some leaders have a misguided notion that focusing attention on the stars will inspire the now-jealous B players to try harder so they can also reap the rewards. While this may work for some direct reports, others may become less motivated, and their efforts may actually decline.

Failing to Address Performance Problems

The one area in which some leaders face a genuine risk of overdoing mentoring is in working with staff who are chronically underperforming in their roles. There are definitely cases in which the cost of mentoring someone into a role will exceed the return. Sometimes the problem stems from "escalating commitment": Leaders may start to view the considerable time they spent building the staff's skills as a "sunk cost" that they need to recoup; giving up on a staff member's ability to learn a given skill set begins to feel like a personal failure on the leader's part. For other leaders, the problem may stem from discomfort in addressing performance problems and/or transitioning poor performers out of roles that are beyond their

> ### Misuse and Overuse: How Mentoring Others Can Work Against You
>
> A focus on mentoring can work against a leader in any of the following ways:
>
> - Miscommunicating developmental decisions
>   - The rationale for mentoring within the team is not well explained or justified.
>   - The leader is viewed as playing favorites.
> - Overemphasizing star performers
>   - Development opportunities are too imbalanced toward star performers.
>   - Weaker performers receive little or no mentoring and become jealous.
> - Failing to address performance problems
>   - People are given too much time and too many opportunities to improve.
>   - The leader fails to recognize when termination or redeployment should be pursued.

capabilities. A leader who overidentifies with her staff or who over-personalizes her role are at particular risk for this vulnerability.

WHAT TO DO TO BETTER MENTOR OTHERS

Finding Role Models

We have described mentoring as a complex, multifaceted aspect of the leader–direct-report relationship; as such, the most appropriate people to help you develop your skills will depend on the specific skills for which you have the greatest need.

In the broadest sense, the best mentors are leaders who have promoted many direct reports. If your organization has a more formal mentoring program in place (e.g., a program that matches junior managers with senior leaders who are not typically in their direct chain of command), strong mentors may have been identified already by whoever is in charge of the program. You might check first with that person for their recommendations.

For help in developing your skills in the actual mechanics of the mentoring process, leaders who are also educators are often good people to seek out. Examples include department chairs who regularly work with post-docs (particularly if their placement record is strong), executives who work with administrative fellows (assuming the placements are favorably evaluated), or senior clinicians who have reputations as outstanding preceptors. Mentoring is also the stock and trade of many executive coaches; in addition to using these skills in their practices, they are often called on to teach them to leaders for use with their own direct reports.

Additional Opportunities for Personal Development

Mentoring is a skill that develops only with practice. If you are not currently in a role where you have direct reports, find analogous opportunities to work with others on developing their skills. Agreeing to work with an intern (paid or unpaid) can be an excellent way to practice and to learn; leadership roles in community organizations can also provide valuable mentoring experience. If your organization has a mentoring program in place, inquire about volunteering.

Attending local professional education events, especially the shorter lunch or dinner sessions, can also provide mentoring opportunities. These events are frequently attended by younger professionals who are actively seeking professional and career growth.

Visiting with them over dinner or during receptions can provide ample opportunities to provide counsel and respond to questions.

Although coaching is the kind of skill that can be very difficult to convey in a book, there are several books out there that come highly recommended. One is *Coaching for Performance*, by John Whitmore (2002). In this technique-focused book, Whitmore adapts sports coaching approaches for use in the workplace.

If you want to work on your relationships with poor performers, we recommend *Crucial Confrontations* by Patterson and colleagues (2005). This text makes a very compelling argument for addressing performance problems proactively and provides approaches to doing so in the most challenging of circumstances.

REFERENCES

Patterson, K., J. Grenny, R. McMillan, and A. Switzler. 2005. *Crucial Confrontations: Tools for Resolving Broken Promises, Violated Expectations, and Bad Behavior.* New York: McGraw-Hill.

Whitmore, J. 2002. *Coaching for Performance: Growing People, Performance, and Purpose.* London: Nicholas Brealey Publishing.

CHAPTER NINE

Developing Teams

Emily's promotion to the role of CEO gave her the opportunity to restructure the senior leadership team to better serve the medical center's needs. With considerable support from the board, she successfully brought in a new chief information officer, a COO, and a chief medical officer, all of whom top-flight and all hired within the space of about 18 months. She now felt the team was set to pursue the board's ambitious goals for improving the center's prestige, clinical and service quality, profitability, and overall reputation as a great place to work.

Her tenor changed just a few short weeks later, when the new team began experiencing serious problems. Each new initiative seemed to end in a bitter and divisive conflict. Initiatives involving major changes to the status quo inevitably pitted the veteran members of the leadership group against the "new kids on the block," and new program initiatives pitted the new members against each other. Discussions about strategic direction started to seem like multinational arms talks. As a result, everything was taking much longer than anyone thought it should.

Emily wanted to support the autonomy of the individual group members, but she was increasingly fed up with their constant, unproductive conflicts. She set aside time at the end of the next meeting to express her disappointments. She made an impassioned speech about how the vision for the medical center, one that they had all subscribed to, was now at risk because the group could not figure out how to work together.

The speech did serve to quiet the meetings down. The conflicts raged on, but now they took place in the halls rather than the meeting room. As more time passed, Emily sensed the members of the team becoming increasingly stiff and formal toward each other. She tried another pass at raising the issue for discussion. When she did, everyone agreed the group was not making progress as rapidly as they needed to; still, no one seemed to have any good ideas for how they could get any better at working together.

The situation described in this vignette highlights a number of dynamics commonly found in senior leadership groups. All members of the group have an understanding of the organization's goals—the greater good— which conflict from time to time with their individual roles as advocates for their departments' goals. This tension will lead to the formation of allegiances, both opportunistic and long-term, as leaders find common interests and opportunities to "horse trade" to marshal support. There is also the dimension of history, in which memorable and regrettable transactions from the past become filter for the contemporary challenges these leaders grapple with.

We can encapsulate this enormous complexity in the deceptively simple concept of teamwork.

WHAT IS DEVELOPING TEAMS, AND WHY IS IT IMPORTANT?

Developing teams means you select executives who will be strong team players, actively support the concept of teaming, develop open discourse and encourage healthy debate on important issues, create compelling reasons and incentives for team members to work together, effectively set limits on the political activity that takes place outside the team framework, celebrate successes together as a unit, and commiserate as a group over disappointments.

For our purposes, we define a *team* as a group of leaders having both of the following characteristics: (1) they have goals in common and (2) their success in achieving those goals involves their interdependence.

This definition is purposefully broad. Most senior leadership groups do not technically fit a narrower definition of teams and still manage to perform quite well. Our focus is not on forming the optimal team per se, but rather on pursuing the greatest productivity with the team in whatever form it takes and on examining how exceptional leaders use their teams to their maximum potential.

WHEN HIGHLY EFFECTIVE LEADERS DEVELOP TEAMS

In the development of a highly effective team, five critical activities stand out:

1. Get the best people for team roles.
2. Develop their orientation toward a common vision and collective goals.
3. Develop trust among team members (as discussed in Chapter 5).
4. Develop cohesiveness between team members.
5. Help team members productively work through the inevitable conflicts that come with group interaction.

With these five activities in mind, we have observed that the following competencies often distinguish the highest performing leaders.

Getting the Best People for Team Roles

In his book, *Good to Great*, Jim Collins (2001) describes the fundamental importance of "getting the right people on the bus." To accomplish this goal, leaders must have a solid focus on hiring team-oriented performers. Strong leaders are very deliberative in their hiring practices; they seek to develop a thorough and critical understanding of candidates and are willing to take the time necessary for making the best hiring decisions.

What distinguishes exceptional leaders in this category? In great part it is their emphasis on the hiring process. These leaders are always thinking about talent acquisition and management, and they will often try to identify talent before they need it. They make a point of developing robust networks of professional contacts, and they keep those networks active throughout their careers. They keep in touch with the high performers they have worked with in the past; those people become their prime recruiting sources in the future. If these contacts are not themselves interested in a given role, they will still be available to provide glowing references. These leaders also make sure to monitor the succession planning processes going on inside their organizations, keeping an eye out for those with high potentials whom they may need in the future.

Building a Sense of "We"

In senior leadership teams in particular, collective goals are a tricky business. On the one hand, leaders need to establish them and ensure they are pursued; on the other, collective goals cannot be overemphasized at the expense of the leaders' duality of roles and individual accountabilities. The tension between supporting the executive team and advocating for one's own staff needs to be balanced thoughtfully.

The best leaders recognize these tensions and will find effective ways to help the group maintain an optimal balance. Tools that can be highly effective in improving a team emphasis include team goal setting and team-based incentive compensation; a balanced scorecard can also help ensure that the team goals do not overpower individual accountabilities.

Developing Cohesiveness

Attending to team effectiveness also means attending to the cohesiveness of the team. Techniques that can help to build team cohesiveness include the following:

- *Increasing the frequency of interaction.* The more teams interact, both formally and informally and both on the job and off the job, the more opportunities members have to know each other as people and the more cohesive they can become.
- *Providing opportunities to discuss group goals, and how they can be best achieved.* Providing incentive compensation goals that are tied to group efforts can also help focus the team toward greater cohesiveness.
- *Developing a healthy sense of competition against other teams.* To the extent that individuals can be rallied around a common "enemy," even if that enemy exists mostly in fun, cohesiveness is likely to increase.

Working Through Conflicts

Every team has conflicts. Carson Dye (2000) wrote in *Leadership in Healthcare: Values at the Top* that many healthcare CEOs try to stifle conflict among their senior teams. Exceptional leaders, in contrast, learn to expect conflict and will actually lead their teams to develop rules of engagement that guide them in their debates and deliberations.

To minimize harm in conflict, highly effective leaders work hard to do the following:

- ensure there is fairness in resource allocation among team members,
- minimize the growth of smaller intragroup cliques (often by keeping the group size small in the first place),
- keep personal reactions out of the bounds of the conflict,
- ensure there is minimal role ambiguity among team members, and
- ensure team discussions take place within the confines of the team.

WHEN DEVELOPING TEAMS IS NOT ALL IT COULD BE

There are a number of ways in which developing teams falls short. The most common are outlined as follows.

Using the Team for the Wrong Reasons

If teams are used for the wrong reasons, they will not yield the benefits normally attributed to teamwork. Leaders may fail to use the power of the many and do not see the value that can come from group discussion and problem solving. Instead, they may use teams solely for "show-and-tell" type meetings, where group members merely report on their individual activities. Another less effective approach is to use teams as congregations, looking to the members to provide adulation and glorification rather than healthy skepticism and skillful contribution.

Maintaining Too Much Control

Teams will not reach their full potential if leaders are unwilling to cede enough control to allow members the chance to weigh in on issues and ask questions. Some leaders place too much emphasis on ensuring that meetings proceed smoothly and without debate. Without these critical opportunities for input and dialog, decisions are inevitably less well thought through and tend to have less overall buy-in from the team.

Overemphasizing Individual Roles

One of the greatest barriers to fully developing teams is viewing team members more as individual contributors and less as team contributors. If leaders place primary emphasis on achievements that are individually oriented, then team members will respond in kind. This can also happen when there is little setting of team goals or incentive for achieving these goals. Superior teams are constantly focused on both team development and on team performance.

Underemphasizing Team Development

Although most senior leaders have had at least some exposure to team-building efforts, too often the approach is event driven; rarely does it involve a methodical implementation of lessons learned into the regular team meeting settings. Although team-building interventions can be informative, they will not in and of themselves build a team for you or even improve team performance.[1] These types of interventions are helpful only to the extent

When Developing Teams Is Not All It Could Be

Team development can fall short of great for any of the following reasons:

■ Using the team for the wrong reasons
- Team meetings are only "show and tell."
- Team meetings are used as adoration sessions for the leader.

■ Maintaining too much control
- Meetings do not allow creative input on ideas and problem solutions.
- Disagreement and conflict is not allowed to surface.

■ Overemphasizing individual roles
- Staff are regarded as individual contributors.
- There is little setting of team goals or incentive for achieving team goals.

■ Underemphasizing team development
- Team building is too event driven (e.g., too much reliance on Myers-Briggs or other facilitated team-building exercises).
- There is no regular forum in which team processes can be discussed.

■ Treating others unequally
- There is a tendency to create an "in-group/out-group" within the team.
- Some staff receive clear preferential treatment without clear justification.
- Power imbalances within the team are allowed to continue unchallenged.

that they are woven meaningfully into an effective ongoing commitment to team development.

If there is no routine way in which team processes and decisions can be discussed, teams will have little chance to grow and develop as a group.

Treating Others Unequally

For teams to work effectively, the team needs to perceive there is a level playing field for all members. Maintaining equitable treatment requires active work on the part of the leader; often there is a natural tendency to create an "in-group/out-group" within the team, particularly when leaders work more closely with some than with others. Power imbalances within the team can also be a source of conflict; if they are allowed to continue unchallenged, they can create significant barriers to smooth team functioning.

MISUSE AND OVERUSE: HOW DEVELOPING TEAMS CAN WORK AGAINST YOU

While many executive groups can benefit from a more team-oriented approach, there is also a risk of misuse and overuse. This can show up as any of the following problems.

Using Teams to Avoid Decision Making

It is possible to use the team approach to avoid making decisions or to avoid accountability for them. For example, a decision that may be best handled unilaterally by the CEO may instead be discussed for weeks on end. Team protocols can also evolve a rigidity that ends up precluding timely decision making. We have seen team structures limit themselves by historical policy; a fast decision might be avoided for no better reason than it "feels rushed."

Misuse and Overuse: How Developing Teams Can Work Against You

- Using teams to avoid decision making
  - Situations that call for individual leadership are overdiscussed.
  - Decisions are extended unnecessarily because of protocol.
- Creating a "country club" team
  - Team member happiness is too high of a concern.
  - Security and stability have maximum emphasis.
- Overemphasizing the need to keep the peace
  - Healthy competition among team members is actively discouraged.
  - Too much attention is paid to treating everyone the same rather than acknowledging diversity in efforts and abilities.
- Overemphasizing the team
  - There is a lack of individual accountabilities and clear roles within the team.

Creating a "Country Club" Team

A particularly dysfunctional example of team overuse involves the attempt to create a "country club" environment—one in which security and comfort of team members become the primary objectives. While the working environment should not be uncomfortable, too much stability creates a stale culture. Highly effective teams, in contrast, will frequently challenge the status quo and will always be on the lookout for how they might improve.

Overemphasizing the Need to Keep the Peace

Placing too much emphasis on teams can discourage healthy tension and disagreements that arise over different points of view. To keep the peace, ineffective leaders may actively discourage healthy competition among team members. They will try to place too much attention on treating everyone the same rather than acknowledging diversity in efforts, ideas, and abilities. Conflicts often present opportunities for improvement; avoiding conflicts rather than addressing them just to maintain harmony will significantly impair team performance over time.

Overemphasizing the Team

Sometimes leaders act as though the team is everything. Their constant references to the team take precedence over ensuring there is a both individual accountability and clear understanding of roles within the team. A lack of individual accountability often becomes a barrier to addressing individual performance problems and is thus another source of productivity loss.

WHAT TO DO TO BETTER DEVELOP TEAMS

Most of us do not enter our professional careers with a well-refined set of team development skills. Team leadership, like teams themselves, evolve to higher levels of performance through a combination of skill development; practice; and open, candid dialog about opportunities for improvement.

Finding Role Models

Role models for the team development competency are best found by joining and participating in a number of teams and task forces. Many organizations use temporary task forces to address problems and tackle projects. Participating in these can provide many opportunities to learn both the helpful and harmful approaches to team development.

Many operations executives are very adept at forming and sustaining effective teams. They often need to accomplish multiple actions by pulling together a varied group of people. Medical services corps leaders who run the hospitals and clinics for our armed forces are also very talented in developing and using teams.

Joining boards or other outside groups in the community can also provide opportunities to study effective team performance. Participation in church or synagogue leadership teams can give you insights, in particular, into managing volunteers and the use of persuasion in team management.

Additional Opportunities for Personal Development

There are many team development books on the market. Some of the better ones are listed at the end of this chapter. However, most are rather mechanical. One unique book, however, is Patrick Lencioni's (2002) *The Five Dysfunctions of a Team*. Lencioni also suggests, as we do, that trust is a critical foundation for superior team performance. Consultant Jamie Notter (2005) provides an excellent encapsulation of the five dysfunctions:

> He (Lencioni) suggests that if team members cannot fully trust one another, they hold back conclusions, feelings, and information (for fear they will be taken advantage of). When team members hold back, they tend to avoid conflict rather than resolving it (dysfunction number two). When they routinely fail to work out their differences, team members often end up not committing to group decisions (they never heard or understood my objections, so why should I bother!). This lack of commitment (dysfunction number three) makes it impossible for the team members to hold each other accountable (dysfunction number four). When the team lets

accountability slide, the natural tendency is for the team members to lose their attention to results (dysfunction number five) and focus more on their own egos or protecting their department.

NOTE

1. A meta-analytic review concerning the effects of team building interventions on performance, the largest ever published, concluded that team building tends to make teams feel like they are accomplishing more, while in reality they are accomplishing the same amount or less. See Salas, E., D. Rozell, B. Mullen, and J. E. Driskell. 1999. "The Effect of Team Building on Performance: An Integration." *Small Group Research* 30: 309–29.

REFERENCES

Collins, J. 2001. *Good to Great: Why Some Companies Make the Leap...and Others Don't*. New York: Harper Business.

Dye, C. 2000. Leadership in *Healthcare: Values at the Top*. Chicago: Health Administration Press.

Lencioni, P. 2002. *The Five Dysfunctions of a Team: A Leadership Fable*. San Francisco: Jossey-Bass.

Notter, J. A. 2005. "The Five Dysfunctions of a Team." [Online book review; retrieved 6/1/05.] http://www.centeronline.org/knowledge/bookreview.cfm?ID=2478.

CHAPTER TEN

Energizing Staff

After another disappointing drop in patient satisfaction scores, Patricia decided she needed to back off from driving her improvement initiatives to spend some time learning how other hospitals were "getting it right." Her hospital's patient satisfaction survey vendor offered to put her in touch with a particularly high-performing hospital in another market similar to hers. During her drive there, she found herself thinking of all the ways this other hospital must differ from hers; for starters, they probably did not have the same labor shortages or union headaches. Certainly, they could not have the same financial pressures. Most likely they were serving a more affluent population, too.

But what she found in the other hospital nearly made her jaw drop.

The hospital she visited was actually far worse off in many ways. Their pay structure was below market, their facilities were much older than hers, and the payer mix was even more challenging than what her hospital worked with. Yet the clinical staff seemed quite cheerful, the customer service scripts were followed at every step, and the patients felt that they were well cared for.

At the end of the day, Patricia had a meeting with Marcia, the vice president of quality at the hospital she was visiting. Patricia only had one question: "How do you do it?" Marcia's answers were incredibly straightforward: The team worked together to find meaningful goals, they communicated progress pervasively and consistently, and they used both success and failure to drive more progress. Marcia was quick to add their department indeed had many of the same challenges Patricia described, but the group had become good at keeping individual needs separate from the group's goals.

This vignette contrasts two hospitals in terms of the energy level of their staff. Although staff motivation may not explain all the differences in performance outcomes, it could very well be playing a central, albeit indirect, role. By ensuring that staff maintain a positive outlook on their work, Marcia is also increasing the likelihood that staff will be willing to try new approaches, give people the benefit of the doubt, and weather disappointments.

In Cornerstone 2, we examined how leaders can most effectively communicate their vision to get people to buy-in and to get excited about their participation. We mentioned the importance of ongoing communication, and how challenging it is to pull off. In this chapter, we expand on this theme, looking at how high-performance leaders pursue not just commitment but *high-energy commitment* from the people they count on. Developing and sustaining a high-energy workplace may indeed be one of the most difficult tasks healthcare leaders are charged with. Success in this area often very clearly differentiates the truly great leaders from the good leaders.

WHAT IS ENERGIZING STAFF, AND WHY IS IT IMPORTANT?

We characterize *energizing staff* as the activities leaders pursue to heighten levels of motivation in the people they work with. Motivation, in turn, can be defined as the amount of effort an individual wants to put into a particular initiative. In healthcare, energizing staff often involves helping people stay in touch with the service orientation that brought them to the field in the first place as well

> **Energizing staff** means you set a personal example of good work ethic and motivation; talk and act enthusiastically and optimistically about the future; enjoy rising to new challenges; take on your work with energy, passion, and drive to finish successfully; help others recognize the importance of their work; are enjoyable to work for; and have a goal-oriented, ambitious, and determined working style.

as helping them see how their efforts are paying off in the service of others.

Leaders have more of an effect on staff motivation than they may realize; it is therefore an area that separates high-performing leaders from low performers, and the highest performers from the merely good ones. Indeed, the extent to which leaders inspire their staff has well-documented positive effects on job performance (Lowe, Kroeck, and Sivasubramaniam 1996).

WHEN HIGHLY EFFECTIVE LEADERS ENERGIZE STAFF

The most energizing leaders have usually mastered the following aspects of the process.

Understanding Individual Goals and Priorities

Exceptional leaders effectively tailor their approaches to differences in individual needs. They know that what motivates one individual can be meaningless or even demotivating to another. A common example is public recognition; some individuals enjoy being singled out and publicly acknowledged for their accomplishments, while others shun the spotlight and feel embarrassed or ashamed if it is thrust on them. As another example, the opportunity to present the results of a successful change initiative in the evening meeting of a professional association may be more rewarding for a single, career-minded up-and-comer than for a seasoned, family-minded manager.

Celebrating and Sharing Successes

Highly effective leaders work to ensure that individuals are successful in their undertaking and teams are appropriately acknowledged. They capitalize on the energy that flows naturally from successes by mining it and spreading it around.

In the abstract, this may seem an obvious point; in reality, this rarely happens anywhere near as often as it could, for a host of reasons. For one, health administration tends to involve constant, unexpected change; the emergency of the afternoon rapidly draws attention away from the success of the morning. For another, the managerial role tends to frame accomplishments as basic expectations of the job; it becomes very easy to view these accomplishments as "what you are paid to do" and nothing more. Strong leaders resist this temptation and work to ensure that recognition and celebration are an ongoing part of the workplace.

Having a Sense of Humor

Given the business of healthcare, there is constant risk of becoming—and remaining—gravely serious at all times. There are certainly aspects of the job that are poor choices for lightheartedness; however, an overemphasis on seriousness can itself be a drain on staff's energy levels.

Many leaders are described as having a very good sense of humor. What distinguishes exceptional leaders in this area is not so much how fun or funny they are, but rather their ability to use lightheartedness to their strategic advantage. Humor can be a particularly potent device for breaking through unproductive tension; it can also help people find the distance they need from a problem to make more objective decisions and can boost creative thinking about challenges a team may be facing.

Beyond humor, highly effective leaders strive to make their workplaces enjoyable. They want their staff to be excited to come to work; they take a serious interest both in the concerns staff have about the workplace and also in the ideas they provide about making the workplace more fun.

WHEN ENERGIZING STAFF IS NOT ALL IT COULD BE

Walk into any department or organization that is low energy, and you will see a group that is not working to its full potential. When this happens, the leader may be contributing to the problem in the following ways.

When Energizing Staff Is Not All It Could Be

Leaders can misuse or misapply energizing, in any of the following ways:

■ Undervaluing motivation
- Leaders do not view energizing staff as part of their job responsibilities.
- Leaders fail to understand or appreciate how they can influence others' energy and motivation levels.

■ Having underdeveloped motivational skills
- A one-size-fits-all approach is used to motivate staff.
- Motivation skills are low in leaders that are too introverted or low-energy.

■ Tolerating cynicism
- Cynical behavior is allowed to continue unchallenged.
- Leaders may be cynical about their own roles.

Undervaluing Motivation

Some leaders simply do not view staff motivation as part of their job. They assume people come to work to earn a paycheck or to further their careers, and they leave it at that. This perspective tends to coexist with poor habits related to staff feedback—staff relations more generally. These leaders fail to recognize their potential influence on staff's energy and motivation levels.

As with most barriers, there is a grain of truth to the perspective: The single greatest force affecting an individual's level of motivation is the individual, and some people will always be more motivated than others. Still, the environment plays a strong role in an individual's motivation level, and the person who sets the environment is the leader.

Having Underdeveloped Motivational Skills

Some leaders do understand the role they can play in their staff's motivation but may have limited skill in energizing their staff. For leaders who themselves tend to be low-energy or highly introverted, energizing staff may not come very naturally. While high-performing leaders recognize this barrier and overcome it by delegating elements of energizing staff to someone better at it, less effective leaders try to energize staff with underdeveloped motivational skills. They typically use a one-size-fits-all approach to motivating staff, which results in limited creativity in rallying staff.

Tolerating Cynicism

Efforts to energize can be undercut by cynical staff. Some leaders will confront these staff about their cynicism, but others are uncomfortable with confrontation. These less effective leaders may justify their inaction by concluding, "everyone is entitled to their opinion," or by trying to write them off, "Everyone knows he's a cynic. No one will listen to him." In our experience, neither rationale is particularly accurate nor is helpful to the team's functioning. In the most serious cases, the leaders may not recognize the cynicism because they themselves have grown cynical; in these cases, unless leaders confront their own cynicism, there is little hope of raising the enthusiasm of the team.

MISUSE AND OVERUSE: HOW ENERGIZING STAFF CAN WORK AGAINST YOU

Leaders can misuse and also overuse their emphasis on energizing. Rather than creating energy, they end up creating discomfort; the result is usually a net loss of productivity. The pattern related to any of the following conditions can occur.

Having Too Much Energy

Many successful leaders have unusually high energy levels. Energy is a considerable asset for enduring the very long and quite stressful days associated with many of the more senior roles. However, if a leader's energy level is too far above that of their direct reports, the imbalance can be a real source of stress.

A related concern can occur when a leader is overzealous in continuously raising the bar. Here, leaders need to be careful to ensure performance targets are meaningful in terms of the organization or department's needs and do not come to be viewed as performance for performance's sake or performance only for the sake of the leader.

Being Too Excitable

We have also seen some leaders overemphasize energizing staff while underemphasizing performance. Leaders with a strong affinity for energizing are at risk for falling into this trap. Such a leader may, for example, err on the side of ensuring the achievement of goals rather than the achievement of performance. They will be sure to celebrate the accomplishment of these successes, but the inevitability of the successes may make these celebrations seem hollow for staff.

Another way leaders risk overemphasizing energizing staff is in the creation and institutionalization of perfunctory celebrations. Celebrations that become routine quickly lose their motivating power; the first award is always the most powerful, and the rest become a downhill slope. Any celebrations of a repeating nature (e.g., employee of the month) should be monitored carefully and discontinued when they reach the point of diminishing returns.

WHAT TO DO TO BETTER ENERGIZE STAFF

Finding Good Mentors

Leaders who are particularly adept at energizing staff are successful entrepreneurs. Many entrepreneurs, particularly in the early stages of their companies, have little in the way of material reward to provide their staff; they end up paying their staff primarily with hopes and dreams. Another group to consider is that of leaders of successful volunteer organizations; success in these positions is particularly dependent on skill in helping volunteers put in effort to further the organization's social mission.

Additional Opportunities for Personal Development

In the realm of customer service improvement, Quint Studer (2004) describes a number of proven approaches in his text, *Hardwiring Excellence*. An implementation of Studer's methods at Delnor Hospital is described in a chapter of *Best Practices in Leadership Development and Organizational Change* (Carter, Ulrich, and

Goldsmith 2005). The story of Herb Kelleher and Southwest Airlines is also a classic in this area. A detailed account of many of their energizing approaches has been collected in the book *Nuts!* (Freiberg and Freiberg 1996). Although not about healthcare per se, there are many lessons from these companies' success that healthcare leaders can benefit from.

REFERENCES

Carter, L., D. Ulrich, and M. Goldsmith (eds.). 2005. *Best Practices in Leadership Development and Organizational Change: How the Best Companies Ensure Meaningful Change and Sustainable Leadership*. San Francisco: Pfeiffer.

Freiberg, K., and J. Freiberg. 1996. *Nuts! Southwest Airlines' Crazy Recipe for Business and Personal Success*. Austin, TX: Bard Press.

Lowe, K. B., K. G. Kroeck, and N. Sivasubramaniam. 1996. Effectiveness Correlates of Transformation and Transactional Leadership: A Meta-Analytic Review of the MLQ Literature. *Leadership Quarterly* 7: 385–425.

Studer, Q. 2004. *Hardwiring Excellence: Purpose, Worthwhile Work, Making a Difference*. Gulf Breeze, FL: Firestarter.

CORNERSTONE 4

Masterful
Execution

CHAPTER ELEVEN

Generating Informal Power

Sheri looked at her watch and noted that her COO, Paul, was probably wrapping up his meeting with Dr. Red about now. She was at an impasse with Dr. Red on several fundamental decisions about the new heart hospital's strategic plan, and she was looking for a way to avoid a confrontation on the matter.

Paul's last meeting with Dr. Red had not gone as well as they had hoped; Dr. Red raised many objections that Paul was not prepared to address. This time, Paul had been preparing for this meeting for days, and he had developed as strong a case for his requested changes as possible. He had researched every single issue Dr. Red brought up in their last meeting as well as a host that Paul thought Dr. Red might bring up. But after an hour with Dr. Red, which seemed to last a week, he felt the negotiations had gone backward several steps.

A few minutes later, Paul called in to report his lack of progress. Sheri listened patiently for a while, then interrupted him.

"Paul, how's your relationship with Dr. Carl?"

"The head of ophthalmology? Fine, why?"

"What I mean is, would you say you have a positive 'bank account' with him?"

Paul thought a moment and said, "Not sure. I think so. We gave him a lot of support when his clinic ran into trouble. We helped him recruit new docs and gave him prime space in the clinic building."

Sheri smiled. "We may need to make a withdrawal."

Paul was skeptical about the suggestion but followed Sheri's advice. He arranged a lunch meeting with Dr. Carl to see whether he might be able to help persuade Dr. Red to see things differently. Not only did Dr. Carl say he would support them, he said he was glad to have the chance to "repay his debt."

Sure enough, by the end of the week, Dr. Red e-mailed Sheri and Paul to say he thought perhaps he had been taking too hard a line with them. He had decided to support several of the most critical requests, although he remained firm on a number of other (relatively trivial) ones. Paul breathed a sigh of relief and filed away a mental note of the connection between Dr. Carl and Dr. Red for future reference.

This vignette illustrates a reality in every organization: Getting things done often requires more than rules and reason; it requires knowledge of the nature of people's relationships and the capacity to use that knowledge creatively. The more complex the initiative, the more of a role these informal relationships is likely to play. Success in building and navigating these networks is another way in which the highest performing leaders often stand out from their peers.

WHAT IS GENERATING INFORMAL POWER, AND WHY IS IT IMPORTANT?

Informal power can be defined as the capacity to influence others without resorting to formal authority (i.e., without saying, "Do it because I'm the boss").

Formal power allows leaders to directly influence their direct reports and may also allow certain leaders (e.g., a corporate compliance officer) to influence people by appealling to a set of universally accepted rules. Informal power captures everything else.

In the classic research of French and Raven (1959), six fundamental sources of power, each with a greater or lesser association with formal authority, are identified:

> **Generating informal power**
> means you understand the roles of power and influence in organizations; develop compelling arguments or points of view based on a knowledge of others' priorities; develop and sustain useful networks up, down, and sideways in the organization; develop a reputation as a go-to person; and effectively affect the thoughts and opinions of others, both directly and indirectly, through others.

- *Legitimate power* comes from the position a person holds.
- *Coercive power* comes from the threat of sanctions. (This is the type of power viewed most critically when considered as a part of leadership.)
- *Reward power* is derived from the ability to provide benefits or rewards (e.g., compensation, praise, promotion).
- *Expert power* is derived from knowledge or special expertise.
- *Referent power* comes from the admiration or high regard that is held for someone.

- *Information power* is derived from holding information or data.

Both types of power—formal and informal—are related to the ability to gain access to and activate cooperation, support, information, resources, funds, and opportunities inside the organization.

WHEN HIGHLY EFFECTIVE LEADERS GENERATE INFORMAL POWER

Exceptional leaders tend to share the following approaches to informal power generation.

Approaching Power Strategically

Highly effective leaders will be selective in who they develop informal power relationships with. They seek out the individuals most likely to be helpful to them in the future. For example, a high-performing leader will typically seek out the most skilled individual or individuals in each department as their contacts rather than assume the appointed head of the department is the best contact to have.

This is not to say that high-performing leaders will only work with the best individual in any department; their approaches to relationship building are not scheming and manipulative. However, in terms of the proactive steps they take to build their networks, high-performing leaders know the value of prioritizing their efforts, and they will focus on where the talent is and where the opportunities for relationship development are richest.

Being Efficient in their Approach

Although the concept of having a "bank account" with people is a popular one, the accounting of favors and support is at best very imprecise. Some kinds of support are more valuable than others, and some require more effort than others. Highly effective leaders learn how to develop these relationships with an eye toward efficiency.

Some of the most efficient approaches to informal power involve a leader's ability to influence a person's decisions on behalf of another person, as in the case of Dr. Carl influencing Dr. Red. The brokering of support, particularly when the "costs" to the leader are low, can yield substantial returns in informal power.

Reciprocating

Returning favors is at least as important as requesting them in the first place. A highly effective leader recognizes the "debt" they owe others for their support and welcomes the opportunity to repay it. Interpersonal relationships typically involve some amount of quid pro quo, or exchange process. One well-known leader has referred to this as "interpersonal economics."

WHEN GENERATING INFORMAL POWER IS NOT ALL IT COULD BE

Leaders who do not have the informal power bases may be impaired by one or more of the following.

Undervaluing Informal Power

Some leaders, even in more senior leadership roles, remain uncomfortable with the idea of doing anything outside of formally recognized policies and hierarchies. Leaders may be particularly sensitive to fairness and due process—and in many cases, the proper channels are the best ones to follow. However, the view can also be taken too far, to the point where *any* informal action is viewed as categorically unethical or underhanded.

A less extreme view held by some leaders is that politics are a regular part of organizational life; leaders tolerate them but fail to see them as potentially helpful tools they themselves might use.

Involving the Wrong People in Networks

Leaders who do take their informal networks seriously may still fall short if they do not invest their effort in the right people. Some leaders do not give enough thought to why they are building a network in terms of the capacity it should yield. Alternatively, some leaders focus too much on quantity and not enough on quality; as a result, their network is too diffuse, and the return on their efforts declines. Finally, leaders may focus too specifically on the formal power positions (e.g., the heads of departments), which may or may not always yield the ideal power sources or the most efficient networks to maintain.

Using Ineffective Approaches

Some leaders are not as skillful as others in the actual practices of network building. One common mistake is failing to recognize the kinds of contacts or networks needed ahead of time. Many leaders build their networks from the problem backwards. Examples include making contacts in the philanthropy department only *after* deciding to embark on a fundraising campaign and finding a contact in employee relations *after* an employee discipline problem presents itself. Although this strategy can work fine for most leaders, we would not call it *highly* effective; because well-tended connections tend to grow in strength over time, leaders are usually in a better position if they develop networks proactively.

In addition to falling short on early identification, informal power will also be less potent if leaders are not as skillful in their relationship development efforts. For example, some leaders focus too much of their energy on the social aspects of their relationships.

When Generating Informal Power Is Not All It Could Be

If informal power does not reach its full potential, the cause can be any of the following:

■ Undervaluing informal power
  • Informal power is viewed as unethical and underhanded.
  • Politics are tolerated but not proactively used to the organization's benefit.

■ Involving the wrong people in networks
  • Leaders do not identify the best people to develop relationships with.
  • Formal power structures are overly relied on.

■ Using ineffective approaches
  • Leaders do not recognize the networks they need to develop ahead of time.
  • Leaders fail to reciprocate or fall short in follow-through.

They may make a point of attending office parties and sending cards, thinking this is helping them build an effective working relationship. In developing an effective informal network, the message you want to send is, "I am helpful to know." By focusing solely on the social side of the relationship, you only send the message, "I am your friend." When it comes to informal power, a year's worth of attendance in office social events pales in comparison to a single, well-timed helping hand on a difficult workplace challenge.

A final way in which leaders' network building efforts can run into trouble is if they fail to recognize and honor the need for reciprocity. This may seem an obvious point; indeed, in our experience, the failure is rarely willfully intended. We again return to the topic of trust building: Good leaders may do well enough that they can be forgiven the occasional oversight; *great* leaders strive to avoid the oversights in the first place.

MISUSE AND OVERUSE: HOW GENERATING INFORMAL POWER CAN WORK AGAINST YOU

Some leaders place too much emphasis on the pursuit of informal power. What follows are some of the more common patterns this is associated with.

Focusing Too Much on Personal Agenda

For leaders who are particularly adept at building relationships, the temptation can arise to use the networks to support decisions that are more in the leader's interest than in the organization's. In some extreme cases, a leader's job security may be based primarily on who they know. In other cases, leaders have used their informal networks to stage a mutiny against senior leadership.

Any time leaders set out to build informal power based on individual agendas, the result can be badly imbalanced networks. These leaders may find themselves comfortably "in the loop" on key decisions and actions that affect them, but they will have far less useful power bases for ensuring effective performance in their roles.

Overvaluing Relationship Building

For leaders who really enjoy the relationship building aspects of their roles, this process can become the end rather than the means. Earlier, we mentioned the problem of overemphasizing non-work aspects of relationship building. We are not suggesting that attending office social functions is poor practice; but it can be overdone. Deservedly or not, the pattern can come to be viewed as slacking or self-aggrandizing by peers and direct reports: "She's off schmoozing again." The attention paid to networking can also take too much attention away from other essential aspects of the job.

Playing Power Politics

Leaders who move too far along this spectrum of relationship building may find themselves involved in power politics. They begin to see the workplace as a competitive arena in which there are winners and losers. Their political activities become a way to stand out and be noticed. The development of relationships and the ability to "call in chits" become their primary reason for working.

WHAT TO DO TO BETTER GENERATE INFORMAL POWER

Finding Role Models

By definition, the people most skilled with informal power are the individuals in the organization whose power is far higher than would be expected by virtue of their formal job title. However, informal power often tends to be a quiet art. The most effective leaders will not bring attention to their informal power, except when it is necessary to do so. However, there are some telling indicators, including the following characteristics:

- *Faster career trajectories.* Leaders who are better at working with informal power tend to be promoted faster. Also, for leaders who have worked in a number of different organizations (or in consulting firms), informal power is a survival skill.
- *Cross-departmental roles.* Leaders whose success most depends on organizationwide collaboration also tend to have well-honed informal power skills. This is especially true for roles in which there are neither legal/policy stipulations nor strong senior-level endorsements to fall back on. These are the people who must truly exercise influence without authority to be successful.

Additional Opportunities for Personal Development

If you are interested in learning more about how to develop informal power, a classic text on this topic is Cohen and Bradford's (1990)

Influence Without Authority. This book provides excellent formulas to help you evaluate your assumptions, consider the interests and needs of others, and negotiate mutually beneficial exchanges to achieve your goals. Thematically, their book emphasizes the principle of building relationships by assuming everyone is a potential ally.

Because informal power is such a mainstay of organizational behavior research, almost any college-level textbook on organizational behavior will provide useful material. A favorite of ours is Henry Mintzberg's (1983) classic, *Power In and Around Organizations.*

If thinking strategically about informal power is new to you, we recommend trying out some of the formal tools that are available for assessing and diagnosing influence networks. The tools can be helpful in quantifying and visualizing what your networks look like, including areas that may be providing relatively lower or higher pay-offs and areas in need of further development. *The Hidden Power of Social Networks* (Cross and Parker 2004) is a particularly good practitioner-oriented text that contains many tools for assessing social networks.

REFERENCES

Cohen, A. R., and D. L. Bradford. 1990. *Influence Without Authority*. New York: John Wiley & Sons.

Cross, R., and A. Parker. 2004. *The Hidden Power of Social Networks: Understanding How Work Really Gets Done in Organizations*. Boston: Harvard Business School Publishing.

French, J. P., and B. Raven. 1959. "The Bases of Social Power." In *Studies in Social Power*, edited by D. Cartwright, 150–67. New York: Institute for Social Research.

Mintzberg, H. 1983. *Power In and Around Organizations*. Englewood Cliffs, NJ: Prentice Hall.

CHAPTER TWELVE

Building Consensus

Scenario A. Alicia was frustrated. As new CEO, she had spent the past 15 months rebuilding the executive team at Integrated Health. The group had been in place for five months now, and although each executive was "cream of the crop," decision making on key strategic initiatives continued to stall. Alicia valued input from her executive team members and did not want to simply listen to them and then make the final decision. She had hoped that in forming this team, they would make many group decisions together. She wanted to exploit the collective knowledge of the team and use the group discussion process to enrich the quality of their decisions. But each member seemed entrenched in their functional areas. Discussions regularly devolved into a focus on turf issues and role clarity.

Scenario B. Hector was overseeing his first budget process at the university medical center. He had given the group great latitude, and yet the last three iterations of the budget had shown increasingly greater losses. The mandate to show at least a 2 percent profit on operations had been clear from the start. Hector called the executive council together for a meeting in his office on Friday afternoon. He stated, "Folks, we need a budget that shows a 2 percent profit on operations. You have spent the past week going back to revise the budget, and each time the loss gets worse. I have a board meeting next Thursday night. I would suggest you come in tomorrow and use the weekend to complete the budget. If I don't have a budget that shows a 2 percent profit by Monday morning, I don't need you. I will find other executives who will reach their targets."

The scenarios described in this vignette are but a few examples of how executive teams can fail to work together for the best outcomes. There are no obvious problem performers, just problem processes. In our last chapter, we discussed the importance of stockpiling informal power, as well as the methods we have observed for doing so that seem to work most effectively. This chapter is about using that power, along with other negotiating skills, to move people toward consensus. In the process, we investigate how groups can better work together in group decision making.

WHAT IS BUILDING CONSENSUS, AND WHY IS IT IMPORTANT?

> **Building consensus** means you frame issues in ways that facilitate clarity from multiple perspectives, keep issues separated from personalities, skillfully use group decision techniques (e.g., Nominal Group Technique), ensure that quieter group members are drawn into discussions, find shared values and common adversaries, and facilitate discussions rather than guide them.

Consensus can be defined as general agreement or accord. *Consensus building* involves the use of group decision making and other techniques to facilitate reaching a critical threshold of general agreement.

Most decisions that leaders must make do not yield equal outcomes for all who are affected. As such, leaders rarely have the luxury of developing initiatives or finding solutions that everyone favors equally. The art of consensus building involves developing the levels of support needed to move initiatives forward without causing some individuals to feel left behind, slighted, or otherwise powerless to affect the organization or other individuals to feel too powerful. Consensus building can be a labor-intensive process. Spend too much time on it, and you have too little time for other aspects of your role. Spend too little, and your initiatives will not receive the long-term support they need for success.

WHEN HIGHLY EFFECTIVE LEADERS BUILD CONSENSUS

Leaders who are skilled at building consensus have the following traits in common.

Knowing When to Count Votes and When to Weigh Them

Not every decision made within an organization requires consensus. Great leaders understand this and will convey this to their leadership teams. They also let their teams know in advance how their input will or will not affect the ultimate decision. Sometimes, they will seek their team's input but will reserve the right to make the final decision. Other times, they will inform their leadership groups that the decision will be a purely democratic process. Still other times, they will ask the group to actively participate in a consensus process to move toward a decision that will involve a synthesis of the viewpoints of the entire group.

When consensus is called for, effective leaders ensure the following elements are well attended:

- *Balance.* As it relates to consensus building, balance refers to the amount of consensus leaders build for a given decision or initiative. The most effective consensus builders do not seek to have everyone agree on a given position; their goal is instead to have "good enough" agreement. They will continue to build consensus until they reach the good enough point, and they will stop their "selling" after that point.
- *Efficiency.* Given how labor intensive the consensus-building process can be, exceptional leaders can distinguish themselves according to how efficiently they make it work. For example, most leaders have a sense of when a battle is winnable and when it is not; however, even for battles that can be won, most of us could improve our ability to know when the effort will be worth it and when it will not be.
- *Technique.* In addition to deciding who to work on and who to give up on, the most effective consensus builders have a well-developed portfolio of approaches to address the *how.* The approach used with any given individual will be well informed by a clear understanding of the individual's goals and priorities, related to both the decision at hand and also

the individual's need for power and social standing among her peers. The most effective consensus builders "make it easy to say yes,"—for example, by finding ways for dissenters to change their minds without losing face.

In terms of the process itself, consensus building does not involve just going around the table to listen to everyone's opinions and then taking a vote on the final decision. Such an approach risks leaving the less verbal or less persuasive group members feeling slighted, and it may create second-rate decisions.

While voting is a quantitative process, consensus building is more qualitative, involving actively synthesizing many diverse elements. While it does not mean everyone will feel the ultimate decision is the optimum one, all should feel their perspectives are heard and considered.

WHEN BUILDING CONSENSUS IS NOT ALL IT COULD BE

Consensus building is more art than science; no one gets it right all the time. However, there are some common barriers that can impair a leader's overall results.

Using a Command-and-Control Approach

Some leaders lean too heavily on their formal authority. As a result, they lack an understanding or appreciation for consensus building. Some of these leaders will stifle consensus-building efforts because they do not view them as valuable. Others believe using consensus building will legitimize others' disagreements with them, diminishing their power in the process. The command-and-control style is becoming less and less accepted; most people want the opportunity to question and even challenge authority and will not tolerate having these opportunities stifled.

When Consensus Building Is Not What It Could Be

- Using a command-and-control approach
  - Leaders do not recognize the value of consensus in building long-term support.
  - Others are viewed as obliged to go along with decisions because "it's their job."
- Approaching consensus unevenly
  - The importance of individual buy-in is overly governed by how vocal that individual is.
  - There is an overemphasis on getting approval rather than support.
- Lacking sensitivity to interpersonal process
  - Leaders lack experience with the consensus-building process.
  - A lack of understanding of the people involved can slow consensus building.

Approaching Consensus Unevenly

Even leaders who understand the importance of consensus building can get themselves into trouble by failing to keep a clear sense of their goals for the process. Some leaders find it particularly challenging to face vocal opposition; as a result, they tend to give in disproportionately according to how loudly a dissenter complains rather than consider how central the dissenter's role is or how powerful his influence may (or may not) be. Leaders do not need to give in very many times before their colleagues recognize this weakness and begin to use it as a tool when it suits them.

Some leaders only seek consensus with those most likely to provide it. Here, the bias is toward approval seeking rather than support seeking; these leaders may have an easier time getting initiatives started, but they will move forward with less consensus, something often reflected in the quality of their eventual results.

Lacking Sensitivity to Interpersonal Process

For some leaders, the consensus building process itself is the greatest bottleneck. This can be caused by a lack of experience with consensus building, a lack of knowledge about the players and their histories, or occasionally a more basic lack of understanding of interpersonal process.

MISUSE AND OVERUSE: HOW BUILDING CONSENSUS CAN WORK AGAINST YOU

Many leaders do overuse or misuse consensus building. In our experience, the following patterns are usually to blame.

Being Biased Toward Universal Agreement

Whenever leaders are described as overdoing consensus building, it is usually because they place too much emphasis on getting everyone to agree. For most initiatives of any complexity, universal agreement is an impossible goal; still, some leaders press on pursuing it, wasting time and energy to push as closely as they can to a universal buy-in. Along the way, they may too quickly redesign plans in a misguided effort to capture additional votes, leading to inefficient cycles of reworking and diminishing returns.

Building Unnecessary Consensus

Even leaders without a universal agreement bias may overuse consensus building. For example, there are times when leaders face

> ## Misuse and Overuse: How Building Consensus Can Work Against You
>
> - Being biased toward universal agreement
>   - Too much effort is devoted to getting every person on board.
>   - Leaders are too quick to redesign plans to accommodate disagreeable individuals.
> - Building unnecessary consensus
>   - Consensus is sought when it is not needed or helpful.
>   - Consensus is sought even when a decision outcome is already clear.

decisions that will negatively affect *all* stakeholders—decisions that no one is likely to support but that still have to be made for the good of the organization. To seek consensus on such a decision is unproductive at best and, at worst, will lead to much effort and time being spent on what is a hopeless cause.

Other leaders overuse consensus building in working with their direct reports. For some leaders, the real issue is their discomfort in saying no to their staff. Rather than taking a harder line, they resort to pleading with them; as a result, staff are extended an inappropriate amount of power in their roles. Although it is often best to lead through inspiration and encouragement, staff still need to respect the formal authority of the leader's role.

WHAT TO DO TO ENHANCE CONSENSUS BUILDING

Finding Role Models

The most effective consensus builders can typically be found in roles that depend the most on this skill to be effective. Internal consultants, particularly those with stellar reputations for getting things done, are often good choices. Strategic planning consultants are often particularly adept at consensus building, as are Six Sigma and Lean Management authorities. Training and education managers are also usually well versed in consensus-building tools, and they may also have some experience in teaching these skills to others.

Additional Opportunities for Personal Development

One of the best ways to enhance skills in this area is to volunteer to lead the strategic planning or other group processes in community not-for-profit organizations, churches, or synagogues. Members in these settings often hold very passionate viewpoints and feel far less of a need to express agreement (particularly if their jobs are not at stake). Working with the diversity of perspectives in these settings can provide you with particularly strong consensus-building skills.

Workshops sponsored by the American Society of Training and Development provide specific group management techniques and tools. Bookstores are also filled with helpful consensus-building texts. Among our favorites is *Team Decision-Making Techniques: A Practical Guide to Successful Team Outcomes* by Kelly and Kelly (1996).

Effective consensus building also involves the use of group process techniques. Readers are encouraged to avail themselves of the many resources that teach the following techniques:

- Nominal Group Technique
- Brainstorming
- Force field analysis
- Affinity mapping
- Fishbone diagrams
- Scenario sketching

These techniques are used so widely that information and instruction on many of these techniques can be easily found through an Internet search or a perusal of any university bulletin.

REFERENCE

Kelly, P. K., and K. P. Kelly. 1996. *Team Decision-Making Techniques: A Practical Guide to Successful Team Outcomes*, 2nd ed. San Francisco: Jossey-Bass.

REFERENCE

CHAPTER THIRTEEN

Making Decisions

After her staff meeting, Carmel, the vice president of operations, returned to her office, still feeling agitated but better than she had felt earlier that morning. She had spent most of the meeting undoing a set of policies and procedures related to unscheduled absences and overtime that she had implemented just weeks before. The changes had arisen in the first place because Kim, one of her managers, had complained to her that the current system was particularly unfair to the many working mothers in her department. Kim had proposed the changes to Carmel, suggesting they would be cost-neutral and guaranteeing that it would a "no brainer" for everyone in the division to support them.

Carmel approved the changes, only to learn later that the other two managers strongly opposed them. They believed the changes would make it much more difficult to discipline staff with attendance problems, and the overtime policy, which was abused already, would be doubly so under the new standard.

The incident reminded Carmel of a workshop she had attended a year or so ago on decision making. The instructor had made a strong case for keeping a journal of key decisions to help her notice patterns in her judgments and to avoid "revisionist history." Given the traps she had fallen into recently, she decided she ought to give the exercise a more concerted try than she had at the time.

When she finally located the "Decision Journal" file from the workshop and got ready to write, her jaw dropped at what she saw. Her last entry, from about ten months ago, ended with the following analysis, in two bullet points: "(1) I have too much of a soft spot when it comes to work-life balance, and my staff know it. I need to be very careful when this is thrown in as a rationale for anything. (2) If I'm presented with a problem and I am told 'all my staff agree' about it, I need to double check to be sure that's true."

She smiled to herself as she considered cutting and pasting those two learning points to the end of today's entry.

We use this vignette for three reasons. First, it illustrates how decision-making patterns surface in day-to-day operations. Second, it illustrates a fundamental reality of decision making as a highly complex but patterned process, the steps of which often unfold largely outside of our full and reflective awareness. Third, the outcome is one many of us can identify with: Having to learn the same lesson multiple times to break a habit.

In this chapter, we take a reflective look at executive decision making. Thinking about decisions takes some deliberate effort, but the effort invested will pay off in improved decision-making habits and higher decision quality.

WHAT IS MAKING DECISIONS, AND WHY IS IT IMPORTANT?

Broadly defined, *decision making* involves any choice between multiple actions or directions. In the leadership context, we restrict the definition to the process of choosing an action or direction that will affect other people as well as the organization.

> **Making decisions** effectively means you make decisions based on an optimal mix of ethics, values, goals, facts, alternatives, and judgments; use decision tools (such as force-field analysis, cost-benefit analysis, decision trees, paired comparisons analysis) effectively and at appropriate times; and show a good sense of timing related to decision making.

There is a tendency to think of decision making as an immutable quality. Although the quality of leaders' decisions does depend in part on their intelligence and experience, it is also strongly affected by their decision-making processes. That aspect of decision making involves learnable, refinable skills.

WHEN HIGHLY EFFECTIVE LEADERS MAKE DECISIONS

Leaders who are described as highly effective decision makers share the following characteristics.

Having a Sense of Timing

At the senior executive level, many decisions are habitually described as requiring immediate action. A highly effective decision maker will have a solid sense of when a decision truly requires immediate action and when it does not. If a decision does require immediate action, strong decision makers have the capacity to move forward with whatever information is available and are comfortable living with the results. For decisions not requiring immediate action, leaders might still act on them immediately, but only after considering whether the decision would benefit from more time, analysis, and/or input.

Evaluating the Best Approach

There is not a single best approach to decision making. The best decision makers "decide how to decide" as a first step. They will ask themselves questions such as the following:

- Who will be affected by the outcome of this decision?
- How much of a role, if any, should these individuals (groups) have in the decision-making process?
- What are the most critical things I need to know to make an informed decision?

The answers to these questions will then influence how they go about making the decision—who gets involved and how, how much time is devoted to the process, and when the decision gets made.

Analyzing the Decision

Analysis refers to the amount of attention paid to the collection of information, identification of courses of action, and weighing of costs and benefits related to a particular decision. Highly effective analyzers will typically be seen as systematic in their approach, though not necessarily comprehensive. The analytic aspect of the decision-making process is typically the most resource intensive; the "good enough" analysis is often more desirable than the all-inclusive one. Taking additional time to collect more data or pondering the planned course of action may often cause failure. Making decisions without complete information is a required skill in healthcare. Leaders who can leverage their experience, track record, and collegial trust tend to be the most efficient decision makers.

Possessing Good Judgment

The quality of leaders' judgment is determined by how effectively she draws on experience and information to arrive at a decision. Two qualities in particular tend to distinguish exceptionally skillful decision makers. First, they select from a broader array of options. In other words, a highly effective decision maker will see more options, including innovative, outside-of-the-box choices. Second, they are more effective in explaining *why* they arrived at a particular conclusion, a point we elaborate on next.

Acting with Consistency and Integrity

Exceptional decision makers are often described in terms of consistency and integrity. This quality relates to transparency; they tend to be better at explaining and, as necessary, justifying their decisions. In doing so, their goal is not to argue that their judgments are always correct; instead, it is to represent their *process* as methodical, measured, and fair. Here, the trust-building competencies discussed in Chapter 5 are particularly relevant. Leaders who are viewed as excellent decision makers will also be described in terms of trust: "I know that whatever she decides will be in the best interest of the patients we serve."

WHEN MAKING DECISIONS IS NOT ALL IT COULD BE

Most leaders have developed good decision-making skills and habits. People would not refer to them as bad decision makers; however, they would not say they are outstanding decision makers either. A number of these leaders could be outstanding decision makers, but they are held back by one or more of the following barriers.

Being Fearful of Making a Wrong Decision

For some leaders, the key challenge is their fear of making a wrong decision. We need to put this one in proper context: All leaders make mistakes, and, from our experience, most leaders know this. However, they differ in how comfortable they are with being wrong. Some can admit it, freely and unapologetically; others try whatever they can think of to wriggle out of appearing to have made a mistake. Such leaders risk losing sight of what is a big decision and what is a relatively trivial one. Decisions involving greater uncertainty and ambiguity will be especially tough calls for them.

Unwilling to Take Risks

Being unwilling to take risks is a variant on the fearful theme, where leaders categorically fail to consider options that are out of the mainstream. This unwillingness is particularly prevalent in healthcare; many managers choose this route at least in part for the perceived stability the career path provides.

The unwillingness manifests itself in several steps of the decision making process. During the brainstorming phase, when the goal is to generate a breadth of options, leaders may fail to lead by example with creative options. They may also step in early to rule out par-

When Making Decisions Is Not All It Could Be

- Being fearful of making a wrong decision
  - Leaders are uncomfortable admitting they were wrong.
  - Too much time is spent on trivial decisions.

- Unwilling to take risks
  - There is a failure to generate innovative options or to take them seriously.
  - Leaders focus on incremental decisions to the exclusion of transformational decisions.

- Lacking good decision-making methods
  - Leaders demonstrate a haphazard approach to others.
  - There is a failure to consider repercussions of decisions or reactions of stakeholders.
  - The approach to collecting information necessary to support decisions is disorganized and haphazard.
  - Past experience and what has worked in the past are relied on too heavily.
  - Leaders have difficulty finding appropriate scope and options (e.g., getting overwhelmed with the details).

ticularly creative or innovative ideas. The move can be as subtle as chuckling at someone for being "way out there" with a suggestion; the message staff will hear is, "I'm not willing to consider anything outside of the box."

In the later stages of decision making, the unwillingness can show up again in how much of a calculated risk leaders are willing to take as well as how large a change leaders will tolerate. Their bias may be toward taking things slowly, giving themselves lots of room to back out later if they care to.

Lacking Good Decision-Making Methods

The decision-making process itself can be problematic in several ways. One surprisingly common example is reliability—the consistency of the process as experienced by others. Even if leaders are methodical in their decisions, they may overlook the need to explain their approach to others. If coworkers do not see the process behind the decisions, they may view the decision making as puzzling or haphazard.

For some leaders, the decision-making process itself is truly lacking; for example, they may fumble one or more of the fundamental steps on a regular basis. For some, the most challenging steps involve thinking through the potential effects of a decision on key stakeholders. While outcomes are not usually fully predictable ahead of time, some leaders are more effective than others in thinking through and managing these outcomes. For example, leaders may fail to reach out to stakeholders for their input into the decision-making process at times when that input would improve the quality of the decisions as well as the buy-in.

"Framing" is another step that causes problems for some leaders. Framing involves coming up with the most useful conceptualization of the problem at hand and the options that may be available to address it. Leaders who are exceptionally good with details can at times find themselves overwhelmed by this step; they may see a decision as a problem to be carefully worked through, when a "good enough" decision is what is really called for.

The analysis step can be another stumbling point. For example, some leaders rely too much on past experiences in informing their judgments. It can be very difficult to give up what has worked in the past, particularly when it is still working fine in the present. The strongest decision makers regularly challenge themselves and their coworkers to consider new options, recognizing that although a past decision may still be a good option, it may not continue to be the best option.

MISUSE AND OVERUSE: HOW MAKING DECISIONS CAN WORK AGAINST YOU

Even if leaders have well-honed decision-making skills, they may not be regarded as exceptional decision makers if they focus their time and energies in the wrong places. Here are some common ways in which good decision makers hold themselves back from better outcomes.

Making Decisions for Decision's Sake

Earlier, we made a case for good-enough decision making. But while some leaders get into trouble overanalyzing decisions, other leaders habitually underanalyze them. These same leaders may pride themselves in their ability to make rapid decisions, and they may have a

---

Misuse and Overuse: How Making Decisions Can Work Against You

- Making decisions for decision's sake
  - Decisions are rapid but lack appropriate judgment.
  - Input is not sought, or it is sought but not attended to.
- Overanalyzing decisions
  - Redundant steps in analyzing options are taken (e.g., multiple sources of the same information or multiple surveys addressing very similar questions).
  - The leader seeks more input than is necessary.
- Being overconfident
  - The devil's advocate step in making decisions is skipped.
  - There is a failure to see the importance of others' perspectives.

---

harder time recognizing how their rushes to judgment can create the need to rework plans later.

Often this problem is related to a leader's discomfort with having anything open-ended for very long. Leaders in this category are well served to improve their tolerance for ambiguity as well as their comfort in spending more time to decide on the occasions when it is warranted.

Overanalyzing Decisions

Some leaders take an overly cautious approach to decision making, using more resources or time than the decision really warrants. Common patterns include tabling decisions without a clear rationale, adding analysis steps that do not clearly yield additional useful information, and asking for additional opinions from stakeholder groups who have already provided input. The pattern can drive peers and direct reports crazy; worse, it often will not improve the quality of the decisions.

This pattern can be symptomatic of a basic discomfort with making and taking responsibility for decisions. Efforts to perpetually seek additional input sometimes suggest that the leader is trying to dodge accountability by crafting decisions as "what they asked for." Leaders who are overly fearful of being wrong sometimes display this pattern.

Being Overconfident

Some leaders have too high a comfort level with their own decision-making skills. The quality of their decisions may suffer because of a tendency to skip steps in the process. For example, they may fail to seek out devil's advocate opinions that would help them clarify and sharpen their rationale for a given decision. When they do receive dissenting opinions, they may too quickly dismiss these naysayers without taking the time to understand their concerns. (Even if the quality of the decision at hand does not suffer from missing this step, buy-in surely will.) A related issue is the selective memory problem, where some leaders tend to forget about or discount how this decision-making pattern has brought them trouble in the past.

WHAT TO DO TO MAKE BETTER DECISIONS

Finding Role Models

If you are interested in identifying role models in this area, look for leaders who are successful in positions that call for both a high quantity and a high quality of decision making. Chief operating officer and executive vice president roles come immediately to mind as fitting this description, as do leaders who oversee multiple discrete service lines or departments.

Additional Opportunities for Personal Development

If you have never formally tracked or evaluated the decision making that you or your team do, we recommend trying this for a while. Building a brief lessons-learned step into your decision-making process can be particularly helpful for uncovering the patterns in your approaches and identifying opportunities to improve these approaches over time.

Leaders with problematically high risk aversion or fears of being wrong can usually benefit from investing time in examining and understanding these fears. Often the fears stem from unrealistic assumptions about consequences: "If I'm wrong about this decision, I'll surely lose my job." Testing these assumptions against reality can be very helpful in overcoming this overly cautious pattern.

There are many books out there that focus on improving decision making. In our experience, serious books on this subject do not tend to make for quick reads. They can take a fair amount of time to slog through, and implementing their recommendations takes no small amount of discipline. For those motivated to do so, we have several recommendations.

An excellent book on developing your intuitive decision-making skills is Gary Klein's (2003) *Intuition at Work*. The emphasis of this book is on using experience to inform decisions and using the outcomes of past decisions to inform future ones. You might think of it as total quality management for your decision making.

A more in-depth treatment of decision making, but still with a practical, how-to orientation, is available in J. Edward Russo and Paul Shoemaker's (2002) *Winning Decisions*. It is a more engaging read than *Intuition at Work*, and it gives a broader scope of application (including much more material on group decision making), though the topics are covered in less depth.

For a book providing more specific healthcare application and with a more quantitative focus, we recommend the popular *Evaluation and Decision Making for Health Services* by James Veney and Arnold Kaluzny (2005).

REFERENCES

Klein, G. 2003. *Intuition at Work: Why Developing Your Gut Instincts Will Make You Better at What You Do*. New York: Doubleday.

Russo, J. E.., and P. J. H. Shoemaker. 2002. *Winning Decisions: Getting It Right the First Time*. New York: Currency.

Veney, J. E., and A. D. Kaluzny. 2005. *Evaluation and Decision Making for Health Services*, 3rd ed. Frederick, MD: Beard.

CHAPTER FOURTEEN

Driving Results

As the new senior vice president (SVP) of operations, Kathleen asked each of her new direct reports to provide her with their most recent annual report of accomplishments and goals. They had not historically been required to prepare reports of this type; fortunately, the outgoing SVP had given them the heads-up that Kathleen would be expecting these reports, and most of the staff had a good start on them by the time she arrived on the job.

As Kathleen pored over the reports, she noted everyone was meeting or exceeding their performance targets. Collectively, the departments were the most efficiently run they had been in their history. In their goals for the coming year, each described raising the bar in a measured fashion, ensuring some continuous improvement while avoiding setting expectations so high that their direct reports would dismiss the goals. The report from housekeeping seemed to be a particularly strong success story, with substantial progress made on the formidable challenges of staff absenteeism and turnover. Employee development was another department describing substantial improvements, including doubling the amount of training provided to employees without adding any new trainers—essentially halving the per-unit delivery cost.

All would seem like good news. Yet when Kathleen emerged from her office, she had a noticeably stern look on her face. She turned to George, the vice president of support services, and asked him to step into her office.

"Let me start by first thanking you for preparing this annual report, particularly on such short notice," Kathleen said. "It really helped me understand some of the strengths of your department, as well as its limitations. Now then, we're going to need to revise your goals moving forward...."

Among the many dynamics this vignette suggests, there seems to be a gap between Kathleen's expectations and those of her direct reports. On the surface, each of the departments appears to be doing well. But from her experience in prior roles, Kathleen knows the departments could be doing even better. She has elected to raise performance expectations as a top priority, capitalizing on the natural tension and uncertainty that comes with her newness to the role.

The focus of this chapter is how leaders most effectively move their staff and departments toward higher levels of performance. Leaders who do well in this area have mastered a collection of skills that we refer to collectively as driving results.

WHAT IS DRIVING RESULTS, AND WHY IS IT IMPORTANT?

> **Driving results** means you mobilize people toward greater commitment to a vision, challenge people to set higher standards and goals, keep people focused on achieving goals, give direct and complete feedback that keeps teams and individuals on track, quickly take corrective action as necessary to keep everyone moving forward, show a bias toward action, and proactively work through performance barriers.

Driving results encompasses all activities leaders engage in to define, monitor, and ensure high performance from themselves and their staff. You can also think of driving results as a set of performance habits—patterns of interacting with others to ensure goals are clarified and reinforced, progress is regularly discussed, and accomplishments are acknowledged and used to redefine expectations.

The habits of driving results are crucial to high-performance leadership; they are often what distinguishes those teams that go the extra mile from the other teams that merely meet their targets. No team is perfect in its execution; to the extent that leaders know what to look for and when to intervene, they will address problems earlier on, making success more likely.

WHEN HIGHLY EFFECTIVE LEADERS DRIVE RESULTS

When it comes to driving results, exceptional leaders can be distinguished by the following characteristics.

Looking for Process Improvement Opportunities

The strongest leaders tend to recognize process improvement opportunities that their peers do not see. This may stem in part from greater experience with process improvement; however, it also seems to reflect a greater tendency to *look* for these opportunities. Process improvement is more a general orientation for this group rather than a tool to be brought out for use on identified problems.

Staying Focused

In addition to their ability to spot process improvement opportunities, exceptional leaders also tend to keep themselves and others continuously focused on process improvement. They can readily bring any conversation back to the ultimate goals (e.g., efficiency, quality, bottom line).

Being Organized

These leaders also have a knack for keeping track of agendas and milestones that their peers may allow to fall through the cracks. The specific approaches differ from leader to leader: Some have an outstanding memory for processes, and others are highly adept at tracking by using a variety of project management tools. Both end up in the same place—more reliable monitoring.

Having Boundless Energy

It is one thing to be described as dependable and productive; it is quite another to be described as unstoppable. Exceptional leaders are often described in this way: Once they set their mind to something, it will either happen or it was not meant to be. Period.

On a day-to-day basis, these leaders tend to see every barrier as temporary, and they look to move around them as efficiently as possible. When the barriers are more indirect, their tendency is to surface them proactively so they can be addressed head on.

These leaders also tend to push themselves at least as hard as they push others. Their coworkers know they will be quick to step in to help when needed.

WHEN DRIVING RESULTS IS NOT ALL IT COULD BE

Leaders' effectiveness in driving results can fall short for any of the following reasons.

Lacking Energy or Drive

Some leaders do not have the energy and drive of their higher-performing peers. A leader who experiences a lack of energy or drive will procrastinate or abandon efforts entirely. In some cases, the difference between exceptional leaders and less effective leaders involves temperament, which is difficult to change. In other cases, however, a lower energy and drive involve internal conflicts that leaders may have about their initiatives or their roles.

Having Poor Organizational Skills

Some leaders have energy and drive in spades, but their execution falls short because their organizational skills are not well honed. In some cases, leaders' energy levels can actually mask organizational problems; these leaders are outstanding at putting out fires but fail to recognize how many of these fires they themselves are setting. Common examples of where organizational skills undercut execution include failing to prepare meeting attendees ahead of time and forgetting to consistently monitor progress on goals that have been set with direct reports.

Developing Ineffective Working Relationships

Success in driving results depends on the development of effective working relationships. Some leaders find this part of their roles particularly challenging. A common barrier relates to leaders wanting to be liked. Leaders who are overly concerned about their coworkers liking them often have particular trouble holding people accountable. They may give in too readily to explanations for underperformance, or they may avoid addressing performances issues in the first place.

Even leaders with a more balanced orientation toward their coworkers will fall short if they have not mastered the art of clarifying priorities, setting clear and well-designed goals, and communicating about them on a consistent basis. All of these are very learnable skills; leaders can master them most quickly by habitually seeking appropriate feedback (e.g., in times of confusion or underperformance, inquiring about how clear the goals were and how well the priorities and urgency were understood).

MISUSE AND OVERUSE: HOW DRIVING RESULTS CAN WORK AGAINST YOU

Many of us have first-hand experience with pushing too hard for results at some point in our careers. We learn the lesson, and we adjust our style accordingly. Leaders who never learn this lesson may not see just how awful they can make it to work with them. Here are the common patterns we see, and their underlying causes.

Underemphasizing People

We have already mentioned the danger of letting a people-focus take precedence over a results-focus. There is ample danger in focusing too much on results as well. Some leaders neglect to celebrate successes and instead jump straight to raising the bar again. The consequence is that staff start to pace themselves because any improvements will only call for greater improvements later. Other leaders focus so strongly on individual accountabilities that they foster unhealthy competition among coworkers, undermining effectiveness when teamwork is called for.

Leaders who tend to view their staff only in terms of their productivity tend to foster attitudes that their work is only a job. Organizational commitment will tend to be low, and people will be eager to find better deals elsewhere.

> ## Misuse and Overuse: How Driving Results Can Work Against You
>
> ■ Underemphasizing people
>   - Staff pace themselves to avoid having their leader raise the bar too often or too high.
>   - An overemphasis on individual accountabilities can undermine teamwork.
> ■ Overemphasizing performance
>   - Leaders focus on short-term wins rather than long-term successes.
>   - Performance is pursued at all costs, and ethical issues are not adequately considered.
> ■ Lacking flexibility
>   - Leaders may push for results beyond what is best for their organizations.
>   - There is difficulty in changing course when necessary.

Leaders with this approach may also too quickly dismiss people who have good long-term potential but who are underperforming in the near term. These leaders may undervalue coaching and other forms of skill development, or they may simply have never mastered these skills.

Overemphasizing Performance

Even when leaders do well with the people-related aspect of their jobs, they may still overemphasize performance. Some leaders have too much of their own self-concept tied up in achievement at work. This pattern shows up in leaders who consistently focus on the short-term win over the long-term success story. Some leaders will come full-steam into a new position, make a bunch of unsustainable changes, and then leave before that reality becomes apparent.

A related pattern is evident in leaders who focus on performance above all else and expect the same from their direct reports. Leaders who think the ends always justify the means can end up justifying what in hindsight can look ethically suspect. Leaders who view their job as the whole of their existence are also at risk for developing dangerous blind spots, not the least of which is a failure to recognize when they are no longer right for the job they have. The classic syndrome of workaholism is adequately described throughout the literature, and if you exhibit any of these kinds of tendencies, you should address them without delay.

Lacking Flexibility

Leaders often find themselves in situations where an initial course of action seems no longer tenable—perhaps the external market has changed, or the leader was working from some misinformation in the first place. Some leaders can effectively admit they were wrong and bow out. For other leaders, the very idea of failure is so aversive that they may instead push even harder on their original course of action. The problem becomes framed not in terms of faulty assumptions but as not working hard enough. Patterns like this can end badly, with everyone but the leader recognizing the futility of a given plan, eventually abandoning support and becoming suspicious of the leader's judgment.

WHAT TO DO TO BETTER DRIVE RESULTS

Finding Role Models

Unlike for some of our other competencies, role models in driving results are often relatively easy to identify because their accomplishments speak for themselves. Within any organization, strong role models will distinguish themselves as the people that senior leaders always want to turn to first to take on large, messy projects. They are also constantly at risk of being overcommitted to things through the nominations of others.

If you work as a leader within a specific type of department or profession, you might seek out role models who have counterpart roles in similar organizations. Meetings and conferences sponsored by professional associations are very good hunting grounds. Look for presenters describing particularly complex turnaround efforts or program expansions. Find opportunities to meet these individuals to learn the secrets of their successes.

Additional Opportunities for Personal Development

If you notice yourself having lower energy or drive around a specific project or process, take some time to think about the ambivalences you may have. The same advice goes for your job: If you feel you are not pursuing it with your fullest commitment of energy, give some thought to the reasons why. Surfacing these internal conflicts can help you work through them, or reconsider whether your current role is a good fit for you if these conflicts are more serious.

If your overall general energy level is simply sapped, consider your track record of physical activity and outside interests. Gaining balance in life by expanding time spent pursuing family matters or personal hobbies may pay very healthy dividends back in the workplace.

If you find yourself challenged by tracking and monitoring, consider attending a workshop or course on project management. Most business schools and many health administration programs, as well as a number of professional associations, offer these. If you are not using productivity tools (e.g., PDAs, software-based collaboration tools such as shared calendars), look to your more organized peers for advice on technologies that may be useful for you to adopt. If you have administrative assistants, look for ways they can help you track and organize your work.

If holding people accountable is a challenge for you, you may need to work on improving your skills, as well as your comfort, with delivering constructive feedback. Working with an internal or external coach can be very helpful in developing and practicing these skills. Also, be sure to review Chapter 7 of this book, "Giving Feedback."

Several books provide excellent first-person accounts of leaders who are masters at driving results. *Who Says Elephants Can't Dance?* describes Lou Gerstner's (2002) dramatic turnaround success story with IBM. Although not about a hospital or healthcare system, the challenges Gerstner faced in many ways parallel ones familiar to health administrators. In *Execution* Honeywell's Larry Bossidy teamed up with academician Ram Charan (2002) to provide a highly readable first-person account of his philosophy and successful approach to driving results at large, diverse organizations.

REFERENCES

Bossidy, L., and R. Charan. 2002. *Execution: The Discipline of Getting Things Done.* New York: Crown Business.

Gerstner, L. V., Jr. 2002. *Who Says Elephants Can't Dance? Inside IBM's Historic Turnaround.* New York: Harper Business.

CHAPTER FIFTEEN

Stimulating Creativity

Staff and leaders of the operating room (OR) were clearly tense as they arrived at the conference center. They had little idea what to expect other than they would be there for the whole morning and would be discussing ways to improve the OR climate. What they found when they got there was an enormous circle of chairs, with poster boards and markers on the walls.

They made small talk to break the tension, until the vice president of surgical services called for their attention. He introduced a facilitator, who laid out an agenda that was almost frightening in its simplicity. Staff would be asked to identify topics for OR improvement that they would like to discuss; other staff who were interested in their topic would then join them in a corner of the room. The convener would take notes, which would be posted on a central wall. The same process would be repeated several times; at the end of the session, individuals could volunteer to take on initiatives after they returned to work.

When it came time to suggest topics, the group was silent for what seemed like hours. Finally, someone suggested the first topic: "making sure we have supplies on time." Topics became successively more daring: "speaking up for patient safety," "making scheduling fair," and even "how about a little respect around here?" and "how do we make the changes we discuss actually happen?" When it came time for the discussions, there was a surprising amount of milling around, people leaving one discussion to join another, and some conveners with no discussants simply writing down their own thoughts.

At the end of the day, the group had a half-dozen topics with widespread interest and support. The vice president commended the group for their creative thinking and endorsed the plans to set up quality improvement teams around the six themes. He asked each of the conveners to have a progress report ready for presentation at the quarterly all-staff meeting.

This vignette describes the use of "open space," a type of large group intervention that has been used to foster creative thinking and shared decision making. While the approach is more common in corporate settings than in healthcare, it typifies the kinds of innovative approaches that can be used to marshal people's creative energies around process improvement. We provide this vignette not as the right way to encourage creative thinking but rather as an illustration of the dynamics associated with a highly effective approach to the process.

WHAT IS STIMULATING CREATIVITY, AND WHY IS IT IMPORTANT?

Stimulating creativity involves two parts: the creativity and the stimulation. For our purposes, we can define creativity as the use of innovative approaches in problem solving and decision making. Stimulating creativity, in turn, involves fostering a climate that is conducive to using creative approaches.

Since breakthrough leadership involves, by definition, reaching new levels of performance, stimulating creativity is a critical skill for breakthrough leaders. Considering possibilities outside of the obvious requires creative thinking, and the

> **Stimulating creativity** means you see broadly outside of the typical, are constantly open to new ideas, are effective with creativity group processes (e.g., brainstorming, Nominal Group Technique, scenario building), see future trends and craft responses to them, are knowledgeable in business and societal trends, are aware of how strategies play out in the field, are well read, and make connections between industries and unrelated trends.

expression of creative thinking requires license to do so. The value this brings to the organization is that the organizations with creative leadership are often the first to the market, and they typically attract and retain the best clinicians and employees.

WHEN HIGHLY EFFECTIVE LEADERS STIMULATE CREATIVITY

Before we define the high bar on stimulating creativity, we should comment on what stimulating creativity is *not*. Most importantly, stimulating creativity is not the same as being creative. Some leaders are exceptionally creative but not particularly good at fostering creativity in the people they work with. Other leaders are not creative, but they still may be breakthrough leaders if they are out-standing at marshalling the creative thinking of others.

The process of stimulating creativity involves the following elements.

Having a Positive Attitude Toward Challenges

Our natural response to many of the challenges we face at work is to think, "Oh no, what are we going to do?" The challenge becomes a problem that we must solve, a worry we must rid ourselves of.

Highly effective leaders, in contrast, are skilled at fostering a positive perspective on these challenges. When faced with a new problem, they are quick to ask, "What are the opportunities that this challenge presents?" and can readily encourage this attitude in others.

Fostering Perspective

Creative approaches require people to be able to view their work from a variety of perspectives—from near term to long term, from the very narrow to the very broad, and from multiple stakeholders' points of view. Highly effective leaders are adept at shifting between these perspectives and helping others to consider them as well.

Consider the "getting respect" topic from our vignette. The solutions this group comes up with will likely reflect the biases of whoever chose that topic discussion: A group of nurses will frame the issue very differently than a group of housekeepers or anesthesiologists. An effective leader would help staff recognize the missing points of view and encourage people to "see" from those perspectives—or, better yet, to seek those perspectives out. For example, there may be a bias toward a recent incident where someone was treated harshly. The effective leader will encourage people to view that incident not just as a case in point but also within the historical context of the department's culture: "What is the *first* example we can identify of this type of interaction? How far back are we thinking this goes?"

Drawing Out Creative Ideas

The most skillful leaders are particularly effective at facilitating brainstorming. Many leaders do not have a highly sophisticated sense of brainstorming; they view it just as asking people for ideas and waiting to shoot any ideas down. In reality, many creative discussions involve active debate about ideas *while* the ideas are being drawn out. The key is the climate: People feel comfortable debating the merits of their ideas without feeling personally vulnerable. Highly effective leaders are skilled at drawing out creative ideas during brainstorming and at discouraging any debate during this step of the process.

Building Up to Creative Solutions

A final quality separating these leaders is their capacity to synthesize people's ideas into a coherent whole. They are able to recognize common themes and trends, and they can effectively articulate them for a group's consideration. They create cycles of divergence (adding new ideas and perspectives) to convergence (summarizing into a new whole) and back again, until new perspectives have been largely exhausted or accounted for.

WHEN STIMULATING CREATIVITY IS NOT ALL IT COULD BE

Leaders who are not highly effective at stimulating creativity will miss some of the opportunities for innovation that their peers may spot first. This can happen for a number of reasons, but the following three tend to be the most common.

Focusing Only on the Presenting Problem

When faced with a problem of almost any type, the natural response of most leaders is to solve it quickly and efficiently. The more pressing the problem, the faster they will rush to a solution. The approach can be and often is overdone, causing some leaders to "solve" the same problem over and over again and never identify the root cause.

For example, one of us knows a leader who has outstanding service-recovery skills. He can readily mend just about any client relationship through a combination of owning up to shortfalls, showing willingness to do whatever it takes to make things right, and possessing incredible interpersonal charm. So skillful is he in these areas that the root causes of his client-relations challenges (e.g., underspecified proposals, disorganization, failure to anticipate communication needs) have not prevented his success. But with additional creative thought, he would probably find much better ways of working with his clients to his own benefit as well as theirs.

Approaching Problems Too Conservatively

Some leaders demonstrate a clear bias toward what has worked in the past. These leaders may be particularly skillful at developing reliable processes but are extremely reluctant to change them. The surest sign of this bias is when a leader dismisses a suggestion with little rationale other than the fact that it has not been tried before, or she describes unusually dire outcomes that are "likely" to come out of such a move.

Underemphasizing Integrative Approaches

The vignette that begins this chapter describes a group of people in a context in which their ideas are allowed to build on each other. The techniques used recognize the power of group construction and creativity. Some leaders would never use such techniques because of their need to control group discussion outcomes. For example, some leaders feel threatened if group discussion is not flowing through

When Stimulating Creativity Is Not All It Could Be

- Focusing only on the presenting problem
  - The same problem gets "solved" over and over again.
  - The patterns and root causes underlying the problems are not identified.

- Approaching problems too conservatively
  - There is too strong a bias toward what has worked in the past.
  - The leader is cautious about new approaches.

- Underemphasizing integrative approaches
  - Creative ideas from others are discouraged.
  - The leader fails to synthesize others' input and ideas.

them (sometimes called the hub-and-spoke communication model). Other leaders view creative thinking as part of their job and will feel threatened if *any* creative ideas come from their staff. In these cases, staff will learn to self-censor their ideas, creating a collusive pattern in which leaders solicit input but do not receive any.

In milder cases, the barriers stem from failing to fully capitalize on creative ideas through effective facilitation and synthesis. For example, opinions may be solicited but then turned into a laundry list rather than an integrated set of themes, or ideas may not be fed back to their sources for further refinement.

MISUSE AND OVERUSE: HOW STIMULATING CREATIVITY CAN WORK AGAINST YOU

There are leaders who undermine performance through an overuse or misuse of creativity. The following are the common patterns we have seen.

Being Creative Rather Than Encouraging Creativity

This pattern is particularly common with leaders who are very creative people themselves—those who might be considered role models if they did not get the process wrong. Some of these leaders are outstanding creative thinkers who fail to "take their staff along with them." They may arrive very quickly at solutions and innovations, but no one can figure out how they got there. They may have little patience for explaining themselves and may not recognize the importance of getting people's buy-in.

Other highly creative leaders have too little respect for real-world considerations. They may enjoy the creative thinking process for its own sake and get annoyed and frustrated when people dampen their enthusiasm by reminding them of reality. While occasionally these leaders may reach terrific, far outside-of-the-box solutions they would not have otherwise been able to put together, the more frequent result is too much time being taken to arrive at unworkable solutions.

Focusing Too Much on Innovation

The pattern of overfocusing on innovation can come from several places, but in each case the process is the same: Innovations are pursued for reasons other than organizational performance. One of these patterns could be called the "excitement junkie"—leaders who push for innovations to keep themselves from being bored. Such leaders may be used to high levels of chaos in their environments and will seek to create this excitement whether it serves the department's goals or not.

A variant on this theme is the overzealous career-ladder climber. Such leaders may push innovation as a way to get themselves noticed. The result can be a focus on dreaming rather than planning or a habit of perpetually overextending themselves and their staff to the point of underperformance on everything.

Misuse and Overuse: How Stimulating Creativity Can Work Against You

- Being creative rather than encouraging creativity
  - The thinking processes of creative leaders are not well explained.
  - Ideas are not well tempered by real-world constraints.
- Focusing too much on innovation
  - Leaders push for change for change's sake to prevent boredom.
  - Creativity is used as a tool for personal recognition.
  - Leaders and staff become overextended and thus underperform.
- Overemphasizing new ideas
  - New ideas and approaches are encouraged, while the mundane day-to-day is given a short shrift.
  - Creativity in staff is overvalued, and operations are undervalued.

Overemphasizing New Ideas

The final dangerous pattern is an overemphasis on the idea-development process itself. While speculation about the future can be very helpful in generating potential courses of action, some leaders are never happier than when they are in a creative brainstorming session, and they are too quick to block out time for these activities. They may find themselves and their staff recreating their vision of the future far more often than is really needed or even thinking through change initiatives for departments and domains over which they have no control.

Having an overemphasis on ideas is another way that excitement-junkie leaders can misuse the creative thinking process. For many such leaders, this pattern coexists with a tendency to view the necessary day-to-day "administrivia" as so dull that it is not enough to keep them meaningfully engaged in their work. The creative thinking process becomes an escape for them, but one that is used beyond the point of meaningful gains. At the senior levels, this pattern can be seen in how senior leadership teams are structured; a CEO may pay far more attention to the creative thinking departments (e.g., strategy and marketing), giving short shrift to other departments that are vital for effective stewardship of the organization.

WHAT TO DO TO BETTER STIMULATE CREATIVITY

Finding Role Models

Some of the best role models for creative thinking in leadership will be found in areas where creativity is central to the role: marketing management, communications, and philanthropy departments are good choices. Outside of the hospital, creative organizations, such as advertising agencies and design firms, will tend to attract the leaders most skilled at fostering creativity.

If you can, find opportunities to sit in on meetings in which creative thinking or problem-solving discussions are on the agenda. Focus specifically on process: How does the leader ensure participation? How are good ideas received? What about off-the-mark ideas? How does the leader synthesize ideas and move people forward? If the leaders are open to it, review the meeting with them afterward. Tell them what you noticed, and ask for additional commentary.

Additional Opportunities for Personal Development

Most leaders can improve their skills in stimulating creativity simply by making a conscious effort to attend to the creative process and by improving the feedback they receive on how they are doing.

A good exercise to get started is to focus on regular meetings in which creative thinking or decision making is particularly helpful to outcomes, such as a meeting in which members are present based on their unique background or experience. Make a point at the end of each meeting to ask the group for feedback. Useful questions include the following:

- How well did we do in getting everyone's ideas out on the table?
- At what point in the process was it most difficult to get ideas out?

For group members who had their ideas shot down, you could circle back *after* the meeting to check in on the effects of that process. If they are feeling particularly discouraged, give them some positive feedback about having a "tough hide" about it and encourage more of the same in the future.

Sometimes it can be helpful to bring an outsider—a "process consultant"—into a group meeting. This person is charged with tracking the process of the group: who is talking, who is keeping quiet, who is supporting whom. His or her goal is to bring these patterns to the group's attention so that they can be discussed and evolved.

Finally, here are two excellent books to enhance your understanding of creativity:

1. *When Sparks Fly: Harnessing the Power of Group Creativity* by Dorothy Leonard and Walter Swap (2005)
2. *Creativity, Inc.: Building an Inventive Organization* by Jeff Mauzy and Richard A. Harriman (2003)

REFERENCES

Leonard, D., and W. Swap. 2005. *When Sparks Fly: Harnessing the Power of Group Creativity*. New York: Harvard Business School Press.

Mauzy, J., and R. A. Harriman. 2003. *Creativity, Inc.: Building an Inventive Organization*. New York: Harvard Business School Press.

Cultivating Adaptability

A morning in the life of Liz Howard, COO of a major academic medical center.

7:00–8:00 a.m.: Liz meets with a group of 15 physicians from cardiology, radiology, and cardiothoracic surgery to talk about the development of a new service line and hospital. During the hour, she rarely makes a definitive statement; she instead spends the time asking probing questions, carefully drawing out the physicians' thoughts to further discuss the potential barriers to cooperation.

8:00–9:00 a.m.: Liz calls in her key operational vice presidents for a budget meeting. She starts the meeting by noting the loss of four key surgeons. She then informs the group that because of the anticipated reduction in admissions, she will need to mandate an 8 percent across-the-board budget cut on expenses. "I don't care how you do it, only that it gets done," she says. The vice presidents walk out of the room with the understanding that the next time they get together, their budgets had better reflect the cuts.

9:00–10:00 a.m.: Liz meets with John, the administrative director of the labs. They discuss his career with the medical center as well as his future plans. She tells him she sees potential for him to eventually rise into the executive ranks and recommends he consider enrolling in a master's program in health services management. She also suggests he join one of the hospitalwide strategic planning task forces she is putting together to broaden his exposure to other departments in the hospital.

10:00 a.m.–12:00 p.m.: Liz meets with the vice presidents of business development and community affairs. They spend two hours together, brainstorming ways they can develop new programs that will involve community physicians and bring additional admissions into their medical center. She provides whatever ideas she can come up with and suggests additional people they might contact, always in the spirit of broadening the list rather than mandating the next step.

11:15 a.m.: Liz's meeting is interrupted by her administrative assistant. Dr. Rodriquez is on the phone, and he is very upset to learn that the lot he tells patients to park in is being torn up and no one bothered to tell him. She steps out of the meeting for ten minutes, listens patiently to his concerns, apologizes for the lack of communication, and offers to have one of her assistants prepare a map with parking alternatives. The call ends with her thanking him for the feedback, giving the follow-up request to her assistant, and returning to her meeting.

This vignette illustrates several of the many situations healthcare leaders find themselves in throughout a typical day. While a single, general approach might be enough to get an executive through these meetings, leaders who move into each exchange with a sense of purpose and audience, and who select from a portfolio of approaches and styles, will find themselves better able to navigate toward the ends they are pursuing.

WHAT IS CULTIVATING ADAPTABILITY, AND WHY IS IT IMPORTANT?

Adaptability in leadership involves the mastery of three fundamental skills:

1. reading the environment,
2. weighing appropriate courses of action, and
3. responding with an appropriate leadership style.

> **Cultivating adaptability** means you quickly see the essence of issues and problems, effectively bring clarity to situations of ambiguity, approach work using a variety of leadership styles and techniques, track changing priorities and readily interpret their implications, balance consistency of focus against the ability to adjust course as needed, balance multiple tasks and priorities such that each gets appropriate attention, and work effectively with a broad range of people.

Let us look more closely at the three parts of this definition. The first—reading the environment—suggests an ability to attend to the most important aspects of a given leadership situation. For example, leaders need to determine who is involved in a situation, what kinds of challenges are being faced, what history may be on people's minds, and how much real and perceived urgency there is. The second part of the definition—weighing appropriate courses of action—involves leaders' judgment on which approach will work best given their read on the environment. The third part of the definition—responding with an appropriate leadership style—involves the quality of leaders' "toolbox," their mastery of a breadth of leadership styles.

WHEN HIGHLY EFFECTIVE LEADERS CULTIVATE ADAPTABILITY

Exceptionally adaptable leaders have mastered each of the three skills previously described. They are very good at reading situations, have a firm handle on the implications of different leadership styles, and have a well-stocked toolbox of leadership styles to choose from.

Reading Environments

An important first step in reading environments is investing the time to do so. Exceptional leaders will think through their meetings ahead of time to pull out the most salient elements related to their role. Examples of useful diagnostic questions include the following:

- *Situation*. What must happen as a result of this exchange? What would I like to have happen? What would others like to have happen? What kind of time pressures are we facing?
- *People*. How many people will I be meeting with? Are all of the decision makers in the room? Who will be missing, and why? What is each person's function in this meeting? How does each person seem to be reacting?
- *Relationships*. How do these individuals get along with each other? How are they feeling about me right now? How much leeway will they want, and how much will be appropriate for me to give them?
- *History*. What has been the track record for this group? Have

they been getting what they want, or are they being turned down left and right? Have their departments been stable, growing, or recently downsized? What approaches have worked well or poorly with this group in the past? Are there new members who need a better understanding of the long-term history? Are there older members who need to get better at overcoming their histories?

- *Outcomes*. How will the various potential outcomes affect the people involved? Who should be recognized as the decision maker? How should these outcomes be communicated, and by whom? How might the outcomes be used to inform our approach in the future?

Understanding Different Leadership Styles

Exceptional leaders will take their read of the environment and use it to select the approach they think will be most successful. Although this process involves more art and experience than science, there are some general guidelines emerging from research. The following are a few styles that appear to be particularly robust.

Autocratic or Coercive

An autocratic or coercive style is a top-down approach in which leaders make unilateral decisions and hold their direct reports accountable to them. "Driving Results" (Chapter 14) is an example of a competency that can inform this leadership style. This approach seems to be most useful in times when decisive action is imperative—for example, when facing a natural disaster or a threat of impending bankruptcy. However, the approach is counterproductive in almost all other cases.

Authoritative or Inspirational

An authoritative or inspirational style involves reaching out to people in a way that gets them charged up about a particular vision or agenda. "Energizing Staff" (Chapter 10) and "Communicating Vision" (Chapter 4) are examples of competencies that are closely aligned with this style. This approach is particularly useful when employees in a department or organization lack a compelling sense of purpose in their efforts or roles.

Democratic or Consultative

A democratic or consultative style involves engaging staff in an action or decision-making process as a peer or consultant. With this approach, decisions may be fully delegated to the group, and the leader may simply serve as a facilitator or as an additional source of creative ideas. This approach can be particularly useful when the staff involved are highly experienced and skilled, when the best actions or decisions are unclear to the leader, or when an employee is being given a project as a developmental assignment.

Encouraging or Supportive

When leaders adopt an encouraging or supportive style, their focus is on attending to the individual needs of their staff or peers. "Earning Loyalty and Trust" (Chapter 5) and "Developing Teams" (Chapter 9) are examples of competencies closely associated with this style. The approach is particularly useful when employees have suffered a hit to their morale (e.g., losing a highly regarded colleague, facing the closing of a program they are strongly emotionally invested in), or when there has been a violation of employee trust.

Standards Setting

When leaders adopt a standards-setting style, they are focusing primarily on process: how it is measured, how it can be improved, who is accountable, and so on. Used sparingly, this approach can be helpful in clarifying roles and goals as well as in improving systems that are in need of immediate attention. Used too often, however, the style will be experienced as fatiguing and micromanaging.

Coaching

When leaders use a coaching style, they are focusing on the nexus between an employee's development needs and the goals of the organization. There is some evidence to suggest the style is used less often than other approaches, which is unfortunate given the high value that direct reports see in the practice as well as its demonstrated relationship to supporting a positive organizational culture. The approach is particularly useful for ensuring that staff forge a long-term relationship with the organization and remain mindful of their development needs as related to their career goals. The "Mentoring Others" competency (Chapter 8) is closely aligned with this leadership style.

Perfecting Multiple Leadership Styles

Leaders who have a sense of the environment and a planned approach to leadership are two-thirds of the way to exceptional adaptability. The last leg involves mastering a variety of leadership styles so they are comfortable enough with each to employ them effectively when needed. For most leaders, this is an ongoing learning process; most of us naturally gravitate toward a single leadership style, or, at most, a couple. Gaining comfort with a broader variety of styles requires practice, feedback, and more practice.

WHEN CULTIVATING ADAPTABILITY IS NOT ALL IT COULD BE

Many leaders are less adaptable than they could be because they fall into one or more of the following traps.

Giving In to Time Pressures

Perhaps the most common trap is time pressure. The dominant theme in health administration roles often seems to be "get it done, get it done!" Leaders can fall into the habit of rushing from meeting to meeting; in the process, they fail to step back and consider the nuances of each setting they are walking into. The same problem can happen on the back end: Leaders fail to do even a brief self-assessment of how their meetings or conversations went and lose these opportunities to gain a greater reflective awareness of the interpersonal aspects of these exchanges.

Being Insensitive to Environmental Cues

Reading the environment is a skill that comes more naturally to some than to others. The natural tendency for some leaders is to be more internally focused; these leaders may need to be more deliberate in attending to environmental cues.

Having a Dominant Leadership Style

A common problem many leaders face is being too aligned with a single leadership style (or two). For example, some leaders are very people oriented; they may foster wonderfully supportive environments but may also fail when it comes to holding people accountable. Others may be very process focused; they are great at ensuring things get done on deadline but may not develop their people effectively and may also have trouble holding on to good people.

Failing to "Hear" When an Approach Is Not Working

A more serious problem some leaders face is in knowing when their approach is not working, because either they are insensitive to the environmental cues or not appropriately concerned about them. These leaders do not seek out feedback on how well their approaches are working, and they fail to accurately read others' reactions—for example, these leaders cannot see when things are "boiling over" or when they are "crossing the line." Chapter 6, "Listening Like You Mean It," provides more information about overcoming this barrier.

When Cultivating Adaptability Is Not All It Could Be

■ Giving in to time pressures
  - Leaders fail to take the time to consider audience, situation, history, urgency, and relevant challenges in planning their approach.
  - Self-assessments to increase one's awareness of interpersonal exchanges are not done after meetings or conversations.

■ Being insensitive to environmental cues
  - Leaders have difficulty reading environmental cues.
  - Important facets of situations may blindside leaders.

■ Having a dominant leadership style
  - One or two leadership styles tend to dominate; these styles work well in some situations but not as well (or not at all) in others.

■ Failing to "hear" when an approach is not working
  - Feedback that a given approach is not working well is not heard.
  - Leaders fail to read others' reactions, so they cannot see when things are "boiling over" or "crossing the line."

MISUSE AND OVERUSE: HOW CULTIVATING ADAPTABILITY CAN WORK AGAINST YOU

Occasionally, a leader may be described as too adaptable. If a leader is thought of in this way, usually at least one of the following associated problems is present.

Being Too Quick to Change Course

Some leaders have trouble "sticking to their guns" in the face of challenges to their approach. For example, leaders using an inspirational style may allow themselves to be fatigued by nay-sayers; an appropriately autocratic style may be abandoned in the face of push-back. These leaders have difficulty living by their personal convictions, which is discussed in Chapter 1.

Changing Leadership Styles Erratically

Some leaders fail to keep a consistent style within a particular context. Often this lack of consistency reflects a leader's difficulty in accurately reading environmental cues. Such leaders should work on reading cues and planning for these interactions, using the methods described in earlier sections of this chapter. Other leaders have trouble keeping a consistent style going because it feels monotonous to them. These leaders may find the innovative and creative aspects of their job to be the most interesting, and they may actively "change things up" to keep themselves more fully engaged. These leaders fail to ask themselves why they are changing styles and to evaluate their reasons before switching to a different approach.

WHAT TO DO TO BETTER CULTIVATE ADAPTABILITY

Finding Role Models

You will typically find the best role models in positions where aspects of adaptability are most regularly required. Typically, leaders who spend significant time working with physicians are quite adept at adaptability. Operations executives are also good role models because their day-to-day working world often presents many unexpected twists and turns.

> ## Misuse and Overuse: How Cultivating Adaptability Can Work Against You
>
> ■ Being too quick to change course
>   - Leaders abandon leadership styles and waver in their approaches to challenges.
>
> ■ Changing leadership styles erratically
>   - Leaders change their leadership style mid-stream, which creates confusion.
>   - Leaders are too enamored with doing things differently and find a consistent style to be too monotonous.

In healthcare, another group that is particularly strong in this area is the medical service corps officers in the military branches. These individuals, most of whom are very active within the American College of Healthcare Executives and other professional organizations, are excellent role models to get to know to ascertain how they adapt and modify their leadership approaches to frequently changing circumstances.

Also, leaders who must have great sensitivity to differences in audiences can be found in marketing and communications departments. These professionals can be very helpful in thinking through the unique aspects of different stakeholder groups. Leaders working in offices of philanthropy are often required to have a keen awareness of history as well as an acute sense of individual interests and needs.

Additional Opportunities for Personal Development

The very best way to hone your adaptability is to find opportunities to practice a variety of leadership styles and to receive feedback on how they are working. The resources listed below describe a number of robust leadership styles that can be learned and practiced. Also, the appendixes provide guidance on developing a feedback-rich environment. We recommend using the two in tandem.

A great resource to start with is Daniel Goleman's (2000) article, "Leadership That Gets Results." This classic article provides a brief, readable summary of research about six leadership styles from the consulting group Hay/McBer. A terrific book on leadership styles related to the organizational lifecycle is *Risk Taker, Caretaker, Surgeon, Undertaker: The Four Faces of Strategic Leadership* by W. E. Rothschild (1993). Each style is treated in some depth, with a core focus on how it relates to developing and executing strategy. Finally, Yukl and Lepsinger's (2004) book, *Flexible Leadership: Creating Value by Balancing Multiple Challenges and Choices*, provides an in-depth treatment of three leadership styles: efficiency-oriented, people-oriented, and change-oriented. Each style is described in a detailed, behaviorally based way, and the book includes a separate chapter on organizational processes that can further support and enhance the effectiveness of the styles.

REFERENCES

Goleman, D. 2000. "Leadership That Gets Results." *Harvard Business Review* (March/April): 78–90.

Rothschild, W. E. 1993. *Risk Taker, Caretaker, Surgeon, Undertaker: The Four Faces of Strategic Leadership*. New York: John Wiley & Sons.

Yukl, G., and R. Lepsinger. 2004. *Flexible Leadership: Creating Value by Balancing Multiple Challenges and Choices*. New York: John Wiley & Sons.

Appendix A
Self-Reflection Questions

THE FOLLOWING SELF-REFLECTION questions can help you determine what areas you need to work on to enhance a particular leadership competency. Read each question and reflect on a truthful answer, making notes as you see appropriate. After you have worked through the questions, review all question sets to determine which area you felt most strongly about. You may also want to use a trusted confidant with whom to compare your answers.

CHAPTER 1: LIVING BY PERSONAL CONVICTION

- To what extent are you driven by a clear set of values, principles, and goals?
- How well do you understand how your values, principles, and goals developed?
- How broadly have your values been influenced? Were they developed by gaining perspective on a wide-ranging understanding of living and the issues of the world (as contrasted to developing them from narrower experience)?
- How effective are you in recognizing when your fundamental belief systems are challenged? How methodical are you in reconciling these challenges?

CHAPTER 2: POSSESSING EMOTIONAL INTELLIGENCE

- To what extent are you aware of your emotions? To what extent do you understand rationally why you react the way you do?
- Do you see the linkage between your emotions/feelings and your behavior?
- To what extent can you manage your emotions? Can you control anger? Can you focus frustration? How effective are you at engaging others even when you are upset, mad, or irate?
- To what extent would you describe yourself as open, approachable, and sincere?

CHAPTER 3: BEING VISIONARY

- Are you intellectually curious? Would you describe yourself as having broad interests?
- What do you read? Do you spend sufficient time reading professional journals and/or articles about trends and developments in business, science, and society? To what extent can you translate or apply those trends into your daily healthcare leadership roles?
- Are you able to analyze data and statistics and understand their broad implications?
- How often do you visit with people from other industries and walks of life to hear about their work and learn from their perspectives?

CHAPTER 4: COMMUNICATING VISION

- How effectively do you balance working on day-to-day challenges with developing longer-term strategies?
- To what extent can you develop compelling arguments for change? How persuasive are you?
- How well can you distill and condense a strategic vision into something that can easily be communicated?

CHAPTER 5: EARNING LOYALTY AND TRUST

- What is your do-say ratio—the number of times you actually do what you say you will do? Would others agree with your analysis of yourself?
- Would others say that you are concerned about their needs and affairs?
- Are you passionate about follow-through, particularly when it comes to getting back to others on their questions and concerns?
- Do you lead by example? Do you help out on routine jobs when you can? Are you a roll-up-the-sleeves person? How easily can others access you when they need you?

CHAPTER 6: LISTENING LIKE YOU MEAN IT

- Are you approachable? (Ask yourself this question again.)
- Do you typically understand where others are coming from? To what extent do you care about their concerns?
- To what extent can you get to the heart of someone's verbal message to you?
- How open are your channels of communication? Do you have multiple informal and formal channels of communications and ways to discern what is happening in your organization?

CHAPTER 7: GIVING FEEDBACK

- How clear and direct is your communication style?
- How well do your direct reports understand their performance goals? Do they have a clear understanding of their performance appraisals, or do they feel blindsided after an evaluation?
- How disciplined are you in providing feedback regularly?
- How well-balanced is your feedback (positive and negative)?

CHAPTER 8: MENTORING OTHERS

- How firmly do you believe in career development? Do you have former staff who have gone on to higher-level positions?
- Would others describe you as a boss who regularly provides them with stretch assignments and opportunities to work outside their area of accountability or to gain exposure at higher levels of the organization?
- How supportive are you of others' needs to attend educational programs? Have you encouraged subordinates to earn advanced degrees?
- How often do you provide "teaching moments"—brief, informal, and unplanned explanations during the workday about a situation or event at hand?

CHAPTER 9: DEVELOPING TEAMS

- How well do you support the concept of "teaming" (as contrasted to dealing with people on a one-on-one basis)?
- Do you encourage cohesiveness by identifying common vision, goals, and threats among team members or by establishing team rules?
- What steps do you take to prevent small, subgroup cliques; team role ambiguity; and emotions from driving debate?
- Are your team members clear on their mutual accountability to one another?

CHAPTER 10: ENERGIZING STAFF

- How often do you show personal energy and enthusiasm about your work and your achievements?
- Would others describe you as goal driven and passionate about achievements and accomplishments?

- Do you regularly use humor, wit, and levity in the workplace?
- How often do you make a point of recognizing the accomplishments of others and celebrating their achievements?

CHAPTER 11: GENERATING INFORMAL POWER

- Are you frequently sought out by people (besides direct reports) for your opinions?
- How strong are your informal networks? How well-informed do you feel through these networks?
- How openly do you share information?
- If others do favors for you, how conscientious are you in reciprocating?

CHAPTER 12: BUILDING CONSENSUS

- How knowledgeable are you about group decision-making techniques (e.g., NGT, parking lot, brainstorming, affinity mapping)? How comfortable are you with using them?
- How effectively do you make use of agendas, outlines, handouts and the like when managing a meeting?
- How regularly do you provide opportunities for all group members to voice their thoughts and opinions during meetings? How effectively do you reach out to members who are visibly silent?

CHAPTER 13: MAKING DECISIONS

- How well do you know what drives your decision making? To what extent are ethics, values, goals, facts, alternatives, and judgment incorporated into your decision-making processes?
- To what extent are you able to analyze and evaluate choices and make the best choice? Do you have a method for weighing various alternatives?

- How knowledgeable are you about decision-making tools (e.g., force field analysis, cost-benefit analysis, decision trees)? How comfortable are you with using them?
- When making decisions, do you hear out opposing viewpoints, or do you tend to focus on developing arguments in favor of your own viewpoint?

CHAPTER 14: DRIVING RESULTS

- How effectively do you keep people focused and on task?
- If team members are derailing movement toward an objective, how comfortable are you with stepping in to take action?
- How regularly can you set a higher bar for your team's performance and help others to see it as an achievable goal?

CHAPTER 15: STIMULATING CREATIVITY

- Do you have one primary style of leadership? If so, in what situations might this style be less useful?
- How often do you pause before an important interchange (e.g., meeting, negotiation session) to think reflectively about the situation and people involved?
- To what extent do you have the ability to read and assess the environment and to develop a leadership style of action that is appropriate to fit that environment?

CHAPTER 16: CULTIVATING ADAPTABILITY

- How comfortable are you with leading people to look at problems with fresh eyes?
- When the people you work with seem stuck in a rut, what kinds of approaches do you use to break them out of it?
- How often do you come up with new initiatives or solutions to problems that bring people together in new ways?

Appendix B
Sample Self-Development Plan

A GOOD WAY to think of a self-development plan is as a business plan for your career development. Like a business plan, it should express your desired goals (both short-term and long-term), your objectives, and the resources you need. (Some development plans even include a calculation of return on investment, as anchored to market rates of salaries associated with promotions, although this is not necessary.) All elements of the plan should be specific enough to allow you to self-monitor your progress. The following is a sample outline for a development plan that you can adapt for your own use. A copy of this sample may be accessed on the HAP web page: www. ache.org/pubs/dye_garman.cfm.

Name _____

Date _____

Part 1: Career Goals. In this section, define the direction you would like to see your career going. It is often most helpful to have at least three anchors—3, 5, and 10 years are used here, but you can select different anchors as you see fit for your circumstances. *Note*: If you are uncertain about your career goals, then identifying them should be your first step.

Answer the following questions for each of the numbered items below: What would you like to be doing, and where would you like to be? What would be your ideal work setting, position, lifestyle, etc.? If you are planning to remain in your current position, how would you improve the way you work or the way your position is structured?

1. Steps I will take to identify my career goals:

What I need to learn	Whom I can learn this from	My action plan	Due date
_____	_____	_____	_____
_____	_____	_____	_____
_____	_____	_____	_____
_____	_____	_____	_____
_____	_____	_____	_____

2. Three-year goals: _____

_____

3. Five-year goals: _____

_____

4. Ten-year goals: _____

_____

Part 2: Developmental Needs. In this section, prioritize the developmental steps you will need to take in pursuit of your career goals. *Note*: If you do not have a clear sense of your developmental needs, then clarifying them should be your first step.

1. Steps I will take to clarify my developmental needs: _____

_____

_____

2. Competencies I need to develop: _____

_____

_____

Competency	How I will develop	My action plan	Due date
_____	_____	_____	_____
_____	_____	_____	_____
_____	_____	_____	_____
_____	_____	_____	_____

Appendix C
Mentors: How to Identify, Approach, and Use Them for Maximum Impact

MENTORING IS A topic that has received a lot of attention in the health administration profession. It is regarded as an important part of developing future leaders. The field has largely taken a top-down approach to mentoring—that is, encouraging seasoned leaders to become mentors, then finding less tenured individuals to become their mentees—but the research on mentoring actually suggests this is not the ideal approach. Mentoring tends to work best when the mentee takes personal responsibility for the entire process—that is, finding a mentor to work with, taking the initiative to work with the mentor, and often finding other mentors at other points in career.

The following action plan is in concert with this research-based approach. It is designed to help you take these steps for yourself.

IDENTIFYING A MENTOR

Identifying a good mentor starts with getting a clear understanding of what you want out of the relationship—guidance on the career track you are pursuing, help with skills you are trying to learn—as well as what you are willing to put into the relationship to get what you want.

If you are interested in a specific career path, identify individuals like yourself who are further along the path than you are. If you work in a large organization, you may be able to find potential mentors by reaching out through cross-departmental projects. If you are already at or near the top of your organization, then professional associations such as local chapters of the American College of Healthcare Executives, Healthcare Information and Management Systems Society, Healthcare Financial Management Association, or Medical Group Management Association are excellent places to start your search.

If you are interested in developing more specific skills, identify individuals who are not only particularly strong in these areas but also have spent particular time and attention on improving these skills. Each chapter in this book provides some guidelines about where these individuals are most likely to be found.

APPROACHING A MENTOR

Mentoring relationships can take many different forms, and sometimes a very informal arrangement works best. However, if you want to get a longer-term commitment from someone, a more formal arrangement may make more sense. A good approach is to simply say, "I am really interested in learning more about _____. I was given your name by _____ as someone who is particularly skilled in this area. Would you be willing to meet with me so I could pick your brain a bit?" Often the person you have identified will be flattered that you asked and will gladly meet with you.

Because you are asking this person for something, make the meeting as easy as possible for this person. Offer to come to the person's office at a time that is convenient for him or her; having the meeting over lunch at a restaurant the person likes can also be very helpful.

When you meet with a mentor for the first time, take full responsibility for the meeting. Come in with a sense of agenda, point of view, and a good set of questions. Toward the conclusion of this first meeting, ask yourself how well the two of you meshed. Is this someone who could be helpful to meet with on occasion? If you think so, at the end of the meeting and after you have thanked the person for his or her time, ask if he or she would be willing to meet again, perhaps on a quarterly (or bimonthly, monthly) basis over the year. If the person is agreeable, then you have found yourself a mentor.

USING A MENTOR

Always approach your mentor with the mind-set that he or she is a valuable resource in finite supply. In each meeting with your mentor, always convey two messages: (1) you are grateful for his or her help and (2) both of your time is being well spent.

TIPS FOR AN EFFECTIVE MENTORING RELATIONSHIP

Prepare well for your meetings

Come to any meeting with your mentor as well prepared as possible, and do whatever you can to honor the meetings you arrange. Before the meeting, review the goals you set out for the mentoring relationship. Consider the successes, as well as the challenges, you have experienced since the last time you met. Write these down so you remember to discuss them.

In considering the challenges, write down enough detail so that you can give your mentor a clear sense of the situation. Also, try to formulate specific questions you can pose to your mentor. These questions should be open-ended enough that they allow for dialog, but they should not be so open-ended that they leave the burden of work to the mentor.

Here's an example. Say you are working with your mentor to develop your skills in physician relations. Over the past month, an incident occurred that you find troubling: You were discussing renovations with a medical department director when suddenly he became very angry with you and stormed out of the meeting. Asking your mentor, "What do you think of that?" is probably too open-ended. It is better to ask, "What do you think might have caused him to react that way?" Even better, however, is saying: "In trying to make sense of this situation, I came up with three possible reasons why he became so upset. Given what I've told you, would you come to the same conclusions? How might you handle each of these?"

Use time between meetings effectively

Before you end a meeting with your mentor, identify at least one specific "homework assignment" to complete before your next meeting. The assignment may be as simple as following up on a situation the two of you discussed, using an approach the mentor suggested, or as complex as finding and pursuing opportunities to practice a skill you are working on. On top of keeping you focused on the skill(s) you are developing, assignments can add continuity to the mentoring relationship: You are giving your mentor a compelling reason to see you again. In turn, he or she will want to know about your progress or the outcome of your most recent success or challenge.

Look for ways to make it a two-way relationship

Although the express purpose of a mentoring relationship is to help you develop professionally, it would be a mistake to consider the relationship a one-way arrangement. Look for ways to maintain a two-way dialog with your mentor. Find out what they are doing in their own roles, what dilemmas they are facing, and what issues are keeping them up at night. For you, this exchange is a learning opportunity as you get to hear your mentor's own thinking process. For your mentor, it allows for sounding out their challenges and concerns and for clarifying their stance on those issues. Occasionally, you may find that you are able to offer useful contacts, articles, or other resources that could be of help to your mentor. This type of sharing ensures that your mentor is getting (not just giving) something from the relationship.

Build in periodic reviews

Although many people pursue open-ended mentoring relationships, adding the element of time can ensure that the relationship is productive and progressing toward its goals. Scheduled check-ins are helpful. For example, if your goal is to improve your influencing skills over the coming year, then it would make sense to look at your progress after a year. Periodic reviews are also helpful when considering whether to continue the relationship and, if so, what that continuation should ideally look like. For example, if you selected your mentor because of her strengths in a particular area, the two of you may evaluate your competency and then decide if you have sufficiently mastered or developed toward that area. You may then wrap up, or continue, the relationship at that point.

End the engagement well

Too often mentoring relationships meet a vague and less satisfying drifting-away end, where meetings get canceled and not rescheduled, then eventually both parties lose touch. A review of the relationship can be particularly helpful in ensuring that the mentoring relationship comes to a definitive and satisfying conclusion. We recommend a final meeting to discuss the future or the end of the relationship and to review the mentee's progress toward his or her goals. This is also a good time for the mentee to express gratitude to the mentor.

We recommend a periodic check-in with your mentor, even after the relationship has formally ended. For example, you might send a card or an e-mail to your mentor a year after your final meeting, and periodically thereafter. In the communication, you can give an update on your career and you can mention ways that you have used skills you learned from your mentor. As always, end your note with a thank you for the help your mentor provided.

Finally, there are three key reasons that many people agree to being a mentor: (1) it is flattering to be viewed as an expert, (2) it is rewarding to help others develop, and (3) the relationship is a useful learning opportunity. Ensure that your meetings with your mentor remind him or her of these three reasons, and you will be guaranteed that your mentor will remain fully engaged in the process.

Appendix D
Executive Coaches and
Other Professional Mentors:
When and How to Use Them

EXECUTIVE COACHES SPECIALIZE in working one-on-one with leaders to help them improve their skills. Use of these coaches has expanded greatly in health administration, and a number of hospitals and health systems have implemented coaching programs throughout their executive leadership ranks. Even outside these broad programs, many health administrators have found a formal coaching process to be very valuable in their own development.

Can an executive coach or professional mentor help you in your quest to become an exceptional leader? While the short answer may be "yes," it is important to first determine whether this step is right for you, given your goals, readiness, and time within your career. Hiring a coach involves a substantial investment in time and money; thus, it makes sense to invest the time in making the decision to pursue and use a coach.

Using a professional coach can be particularly helpful in these two circumstances:

1. Someone has expressed concern about a deficit in your leadership skills.
2. You are preparing for a specific position that requires substantively different leadership skills than you currently possess.

Both of these circumstances are specific. A coach should be able to help you determine the needed competencies and identify goals to work toward.

IDENTIFYING COMPETENCIES YOU WANT TO DEVELOP

If you have specific developmental goals, the next step is to determine the competencies you need to master to achieve your goals. A performance evaluation, a 360-degree feedback program (see Appendix F), or other developmental programs can be good sources for identifying the areas that you need to improve.

In general, coaching is most useful for developing the competencies for which other development options are not readily available—either the role models just are not there or they cannot take the time to work with you. Additionally, the more opportunities you have to practice a given competency on the job, the more effective coaching is in helping you develop your skills rapidly. The converse is also true, however: Coaching will do little good if you are not gaining the work experience at the same time.

DETERMINING YOUR PERSONAL READINESS

A good coach is supportive but is also able to challenge you in the no-pain, no-gain sense of the word. Not everyone does well with this type of feedback. Some people find it too disconcerting and thus have trouble hearing it (the "listening like you mean it" competency is particularly relevant here). Kilburg (2001) provides some diagnostic questions that, with a little adaptation, can work well in assessing your own readiness to be coached:

1. How *personally* motivated are you to develop these competencies? Is this something you want for yourself, or are you doing it

mostly to appease someone else (e.g., a superior, spouse)?

2. Have you tried to work on these competencies before? If so, what have you tried, and how long were you able to stick with the approach?
3. What concerns do you have about being coached? How optimistic/pessimistic are you about its potential results?
4. Have you ever had problems following through on developmental assignments in the past?
5. How easy/difficult do you find it to accept constructive feedback?
6. How often have you given up on things because they became too personally challenging?

If you have trouble with constructive feedback, give up on efforts that become too personally challenging, have trouble with follow through, or are pursuing coaching for reasons outside of yourself, then you are much less likely to see positive outcomes from a coaching engagement. Conversely, if you tend to be tenacious in following goals, are able to wince your way through constructive feedback, and are doing this for yourself, you are much more likely to see successful results.

FINDING AND SELECTING A COACH

Some words of caution are in order here. Despite what some organizations may say, there is no widely recognized certification for expertise in coaching (Garman, Whiston, and Zlatoper 2001). In fact, as of this writing, the opinion of many in the profession is that the existing certifications have no relationship with expertise whatsoever. In short, screen coaches cautiously and do not mistake a coaching-branded credential for effectiveness.

In general, the best source for coaches is a personal referral. You may ask colleagues who have worked with coaches to recommend someone; you may also ask them specific questions such as the coach's experience, style, and availability. Another good source of referral may be the vice president of human resources in your organization.

If you want to broaden your search, the American College of Healthcare Executives maintains the Executive Coaches Directory Guide. The guide lists coaches who are affiliated with ACHE and provides an in-depth description of the nature of their practice, approach, and fee structure. While it is a directory and not a screening tool, the guide is a starting point for identifying potential coaching resources. It is searchable by several fields, including practice location—see http://www.ache.org/newclub/career/execcoach/intro.cfm.

We strongly recommend that you interview at least two, but preferably three or more, coaches. You should feel free to ask any questions about the coach's experience, approach, and fee structure before you get started on the process. If a coach tries to dodge your questions or hard-sell you, look for someone else.

Questions for Screening a Coach

How did you come to be a coach? How did you prepare for this role?
As previously noted, there is no recognized certification for coaching. However, it is still useful to find out how a coach has prepared for his or her role, and some training certainly carries more weight than others. For example, if a coach has a doctoral degree in adult education or psychology, he or she likely has a much deeper fund of process skills to draw from than someone whose sole credentials involve experience. Ask for details if a coach states he or she attended a training program (e.g., how long, what was involved).

How long have you been working as a coach? How much coaching do you do?
Many coaches do not practice coaching full time. In general, however, more experience as a coach means better skills.

What kinds of positions have you coached?
You should favor coaches who have experience working at *and* above your current level in the organization.

How much of your work is focused in healthcare? What kinds of healthcare organizations?
Experience in the field may be more or less important, depending on the specific competencies you wish to develop. In general, however, a coach with relevant experience may better understand the complex environment healthcare administrators face.

What kind of work did you do before you became a coach (e.g., amount of time on the job, organization type, position level/span of control)?
All else equal, coaches who have worked as leaders themselves will have a better-developed mental model of the leadership challenges you face.

How would you describe your approach to coaching? Do you a have particular area of focus or expertise?
As a coach responds to these two questions, ask yourself whether the approach sounds clear, reasonable, effective, and something you will be comfortable with. However, be cautious of coaches who seem overly enamored with their models or who seem to love to talk.

What types of engagements/arrangements will you work with?
There are no standard fees in coaching, and coach arrangements are somewhat all over the map. The most typical arrangements are flat-fee retainer (often for a 6- or 12-month contract), day rate (essentially an hourly rate billed in 8-hour blocks), hourly, and per session.

Can you provide client references?
While references can be very helpful, some coaches (especially psychologists and other behavioral health professionals) do not provide client references because of concerns about client confidentiality. Sometimes in these cases, a coach will, if asked, provide the name of a general contact (e.g., a vice president of HR) from a client's organi-

zation who can comment more generally about the coach's services.

OTHER CONSIDERATIONS

1. Coaching is a relationship, and you get what you give. A coach cannot do the work for you; if you do not take the work seriously, you will not get the maximum value out of the consultation.
2. Coaching takes time (sometimes a lot of time) to yield results. If you are working on changing fundamental aspects of the way you work with others, you should plan on being involved with the coach for at least 12 months before you can observe significant results.

REFERENCES

Garman, A. N., D. L. Whiston, and K. W. Zlatoper. 2000. "Media Perceptions of Executive Coaching and the Formal Preparation of Coaches." *Consulting Psychology Journal* 52: 201-05.

Kilburg. 2001. "Facilitating Intervention Adherence in Executive Coaching: A Model and Methods." *Consulting Psychology Journal* 53: 251-67.

Appendix E
Action Plan: Developing a Feedback-Rich Working Environment

THROUGHOUT THE BOOK we highlight the value of cultivating a feedback-rich working environment, to which you may have thought, "easier said than done!" Indeed, changing the level of feedback in your working environment sometimes requires the transformation of the organizational or departmental culture. This can be done, and its rewards are substantial.

The techniques that follow are proven to improve feedback within a healthcare environment. They are listed roughly in order of the depth of feedback they can yield; the first techniques are the most straightforward to implement. The best approach for each technique is to lead by example—that is, first implement the technique yourself, then encourage your staff to adopt it. Continue this process until it becomes the habit within your team.

THE TWO-STEP PROCESS REVIEW

This technique is best implemented immediately after a given performance. Examples include a presentation before an important group, a negotiation session with a vendor, or a joint meeting with a patient's family. In this technique, the principal performer (e.g., the person managing the presentation, facilitating the meeting) is first asked to comment on his or her own performance in two steps. First, the person is asked to describe what he or she thought went particularly well in the performance. Second, the person is asked what he or she would do differently if given a chance to do the performance over again. This self-assessment is then followed by soliciting feedback from those who observed the performance using the same questioning format (what went well, what could be done differently).

The two-step process review serves several goals. By starting with the performer's perceptions, the feedback providers are in the best position to tailor their comments to the performer's understanding of his or her own performance. Also, the feedback is more likely to be viewed as value-added knowledge rather than redundant information (or what the performer already knows).

DEVELOPING A SHARED LANGUAGE ABOUT COMPETENCIES

In environments where performance-related discussions are not taking place frequently, staff may not have a good fund of performance "language" to work with or good feedback skills with which to deliver performance information. By meeting as a group to develop shared competencies, you can help staff develop their own language and reach a comfort level with it. If these meetings are developed in a climate of sufficient psychological safety, they can over time turn into process improvement meetings in which performance-related dialog is present.

360-DEGREE FEEDBACK

A developmentally focused 360-degree feedback program is also an effective way to enlist a department in having more frequent performance-related discussions. These programs work particularly well after a team has developed a shared sense of competencies. Appendix F describes these programs in greater depth.

SHARING INDIVIDUAL GOALS

Too often, individual developmental goals are perceived to be blemishes: We recognize the need to work on them, but we also do our best to hide them from the rest of the world. Sharing of individual goals, while uncomfortable at first, is often a more robust approach to making meaningful strides in improvements. For example, a director who has been told that he occasionally delivers critiques in a harsh and demoralizing way may be able to improve by simply being mindful of his emotions. However, he will improve much faster if he articulates his developmental goal to his direct reports. In doing so, he gives himself an opportunity to get feedback from those who are most familiar with his performance. For example, he may say to a staff member after giving her feedback, "As you know I am working on delivering constructive feedback in a more even fashion. How did you think that went?"

PERFORMANCE CALIBRATION MEETING

Even leaders who are highly experienced in providing feedback can start to drift into their own unique interpretations of performance. For example, taking two weeks to resolve a payroll issue may seem acceptable to one leader but may be incredibly insensitive to another.

Leaders can help each other refine their internal "yardsticks" through a process of performance calibration. The process involves leaders within a particular department or service line having a dialog about how staff are being rated on performance appraisals. The idea is to show one another how they rate employees and to get each other's opinions on whether the ratings and rationales are about right, too generous, or too harsh. Through this process, leaders have an opportunity to refine their own thinking by hearing from their peers and to view and discuss performance in new ways.

TALENT REVIEW

A talent review is a periodic meeting of leaders to discuss employee performance levels vis-à-vis current and emerging organizational needs. Many different approaches to the talent review process exist, but all of them typically involve discussing questions about the fit of a certain employee for a specific current or future role. Like calibration meetings, talent reviews can afford leaders the opportunity to check their own thinking about performance against that of their peers. Additionally, the process provides a forum for discussing performance-related needs at the broader organizational and strategic levels. They also help to promote the perspective that leaders are not expected to occupy a role forever, but rather they should be preparing for transition and succession.

While a talent review process can provide many benefits, its implementation is not to be taken lightly. Because talent reviews involve active discussions about whether a person is right for a role, they tend to be the most threatening. Talent reviews usually require top-level support, and occasionally a major culture change, to implement.

Appendix F
Action Plan: Implementing a 360-Degree Feedback Program

360-DEGREE FEEDBACK programs involve soliciting feedback from a variety of actors surrounding a role—peers, direct reports, superiors, clients, to name a few—and then providing that feedback to the person being reviewed in a way that masks the source of the feedback.

Following are the eight major steps in a 360-degree feedback process, including the associated decisions that need to be made and current thoughts on best practices in each step.

STEP 1: DEFINE THE PARTICIPANTS AND THE GOALS

360-degree feedback can be implemented for a single leader, a team of leaders, or the leadership of a whole organization. If broad participation is sought, it is often best to start at the top of the organization and move down from there; this allows senior-level executives to gain familiarity with the process first and to lead by example.

In terms of goals, the main decision that needs to be made is whether the process is used for development or for appraisal (e.g., will the feedback have an impact on the participant's formal performance evaluation). In general, 360-degree feedback programs are most useful when used strictly for developmental purposes; this means that the only ones allowed to view the results are the leader and the feedback facilitator. If used for appraisal purposes, these programs tend to fall prey to the same biases that cloud regular performance appraisals (Eichenger and Lombardo 2003). In short, they cannot serve both purposes and tend to serve the developmental goal better.

STEP 2: DEVELOP (OR IDENTIFY) THE SURVEY INSTRUMENT

The survey instrument used should, foremost, serve the needs of the people who agreed to participate in the feedback process. While there are many off-the-shelf surveys out there, these surveys often prove to be an awkward fit when it comes to a specific application for certain leadership roles. Some competencies may be relevant and on target, while others may be irrelevant or not as important. For this reason, many organizations elect to either develop their own survey or modify an existing one. (Items from the Health Administrators Leadership survey described in Garman, Tyler, and Darnall (2004) can be used and modified royalty-free for noncommercial purposes. The item list that article refers to can be obtained through http://www.liacus.com/free_resources/index.htm.)

Here are general rules-of-thumb for survey development:

It is tempting to throw "everything but the kitchen sink" onto a survey, but in reality less is often more. A range of 35-60 items is often reasonable. The higher above that upper item limit goes, the less thought people put into their responses to each item.

Always include space for open-ended comments, and encourage (or mandate) their use. The open-ended feedback often contains the most useful data a person receives in this process.

STEP 3: DECIDE HOW TO MANAGE THE PROCESS

Internet-hosted surveys are the preferred choice from an efficiency perspective. Systems from online survey vendors (e.g., Surveymonkey.com) can provide low and even no-cost options, particularly for small-scale projects. Specialty vendors provide options for larger-scale projects; prices vary widely so it is useful to comparison shop.

We strongly encourage you to use an outside person to handle the data-management portion of any 360-degree project. Given the potentially highly sensitive nature of the feedback, being able to ensure confidentiality in both fact and appearance is very important. The outside person does not necessarily have to be outside of your organization. For example, if you have a relatively sophisticated employee/organization development group in-house, the group may have the capabilities to manage such a project.

If you do go outside the organization for assistance, consider contacting the industrial psychology department of your local university. The school may have an academic consulting group that can provide high-quality oversight at a fraction of what private-sector consultants charge.

STEP 4: IDENTIFY FEEDBACK SOURCES

All participants in a 360-degree feedback process need to reach out to the individuals they work with to solicit feedback. It is very helpful to set, ahead of time, the parameters for the process—who to ask to participate (e.g., peers, superiors, direct reports), how many participants to solicit, and/or whether to allow anyone who wishes to participate.

Here are general rules-of-thumb for setting participant parameters:

- If people choose their own raters, encourage them to include people (colleagues, direct reports, supervisors) they do not work well or even have a conflict with. From these individuals, they often learn the most about themselves and their limitations.

- More feedback providers tend to be better than a fewer number of participants. This way, the "signal" has a better chance of rising above the "noise."

STEP 5: DISTRIBUTE/ COLLECT THE SURVEY

Set a deadline for feedback, but anticipate that you will need to extend it at least once and likely twice. Depending on how the distribution/collection process is being managed, the survey process can be wrapped up in as little as two weeks or as long as four or more.

STEP 6: DEVELOP THE REPORTS

With online systems, the development of feedback reports can be an automatic or semiautomatic process. However, distributing print copies is still helpful as they are more likely to be kept for later review or reference.

STEP 7: PROVIDE FEEDBACK AND FORMULATE DEVELOPMENTAL PLANS

Feedback can be delivered in a number of ways. At one extreme is the "desk drop," in which a person receives his or her report without being given a chance for discussion or any expectation for follow-up. At the other extreme is a facilitated meeting between the person, a feedback coach, and the person's superior to discuss the results, brainstorm developmental plans, and set specific improvement goals and a timeline for follow-up.

In our experience, the approach that works best is to have a feedback facilitator (again, usually someone outside the person's immediate chain of command) meet with the individual to go over the feedback results and think through the implications for development. These meetings typically take at least 60 minutes on average, but this investment in time is worth it as it improves the person's feedback receptivity and clarifies his or her developmental plans.

STEP 8: FOLLOW-UP

People participating in a non-self-initiated 360-degree process should have specific expectations for using their results. At a minimum, the participant should discuss with his or her superior the development plan they created together. Additionally, the participant should follow-up with people who provided feedback. For example, a participant may address his or her staff during a staff meeting not only to express gratitude for their participation but also to note the areas of strength and developmental needs the report revealed. The participant may also share his or her plans to address the areas identified and request the staff to continue giving him or her feedback on progress. Taking this extra step serves three goals: (1) it demonstrates the leader's receptivity to his or her direct reports' feedback, (2) it role-models good feedback-receiving behavior, and (3) it holds the leader publicly accountable for making progress.

In terms of tracking progress, leaders are often interested in readministering the 360-degree feedback to look at change over time. Although this can sometimes be helpful, it is often equally effective (and less labor intensive) to simply ask colleagues and staff whether they have noticed change in the areas of interest. This approach also serves to encourage a feedback-rich work environment.

REFERENCES

Eichenger, R. W., and M. M. Lombardo. 2003. "Knowledge Summary Series: 360-Degree Assessment." *Human Resource Planning* 26: 34-44.

Garman, A. N., J. L. Tyler, and J. S. Darnall. 2004. "Development and Validation of a 360-Degree Feedback Instrument for Healthcare Administrators." *Journal of Healthcare Management* 49 (5): 307-22.

About the Authors

CARSON F. DYE, M.B.A., FACHE, is a management and search consultant with Witt/Kieffer who conducts chief executive officer, senior executive, and physician executive searches for a variety of healthcare organizations. His consulting experience includes leadership assessment, organizational design, and leadership development. He also assists boards  in executive and physician compensation, conducts board retreats, and provides counsel in chief executive officers' employment contracts and evaluation matters for a variety of client organizations. He is certified to work with the Hogan Assessment Systems tools for selection, development, and executive coaching.

Prior to entering executive search, Mr. Dye was a principal and director of Findley Davies, Inc.'s Health Care Industry Consulting Division. Prior to his consulting career, he served 20 years as chief human resources officer at various organizations, including St. Vincent Medical Center, Ohio State University Medical Center, Children's Hospital Medical Center, and Clermont Mercy Hospital.

Mr. Dye has been named as a physician leadership consultant expert on the LaRoche National Consultant Panel and is a member of the Governance Institute Governance One Hundred. He works as a special advisor to The Healthcare Roundtable. He also serves on the faculty of the graduate program in management and health services policy at Ohio State University.

Since 1989, Mr. Dye has taught several cluster programs for the American College of Healthcare Executives and frequently speaks for state and local hospital associations. He authored the 2001 James A. Hamilton Book of the Year Award winner, *Leadership in Healthcare: Values at the Top* (Health Administration Press 2000). In addition, he has written *Winning the Talent War: Ensuring Effective Leadership in Healthcare* (Health Administration Press 2002), *Executive Excellence* (Health Administration Press 2000), and *Protocols for Health Care Executive Behavior* (Health Administration Press 1993). He has also written several professional journal articles on leadership and human resources.

Mr. Dye has had a life-long interest in leadership and its impact on organizations. He has studied how values drive leadership and affect change management. He is also a student of executive assessment and selection.

Mr. Dye earned his B.A. from Marietta College and his M.B.A. from Xavier University.

ANDREW N. GARMAN, PSY.D., M.S., is associate chair and director of master's programs in the Department of Health Systems Management at Rush University in Chicago. In his practitioner role, Dr. Garman provides a variety of leadership assessment and development services, including the development of assessment centers, tests, 360-degree feedback, surveys, and work-  shops. In his work with the Rush University Medical Center, he teaches graduate courses on topics, including governance, leadership, ethics, professionalism, decision sciences, organizational analysis and change management, and entrepreneurship. He also serves as associate editor for the *Consulting Psychology Journal* and cochairs the Human Resource Faculty Forum of the Association of University Programs in Health Administration.

Dr. Garman is a recognized authority in evidence-based leadership assessment and development practice. His research and applied work have been published in more than 25 peer-reviewed journals and books. For his work in leadership competency modeling and CEO succession planning, he received three Health Management Research Awards from the American College of Healthcare Executives.

Dr. Garman's prior work experience includes a variety of practitioner and faculty roles with organizations, including the Federal Reserve Bank of Chicago, the Illinois Institute of Technology, and the University of Chicago.

Dr. Garman received his B.S. in psychology/mathematics emphasis from Pennsylvania State University, his M.S. in personnel and human resource development from the Illinois Institute of Technology, and his Psy.D. in clinical psychology from the College of William & Mary/Virginia Consortium. Dr. Garman is also an Illinois-licensed clinical psychologist.